Miracle On Buffalo Pass
Rocky Mountain Airways
Flight 217

Harrison Jones

Best Wishes,
Harrison Jones.

Gary M Cole
1ST officer

Bruce + Korri

Not in many books so
I don't sign them much.
So, I guess I'm supposed to
say something here." Hope you
can read". Anyway.
Signed by Harrison + my Bro.
Harrison has become a close
family friend & worked hard on
this project. His daughter Kelly
came up with the idea that this
event deserved a book.

Your friend in
Skiing Adventures

Miracle on Buffalo Pass
Rocky Mountain Airways
Flight 217

ISBN-13: 978-0692886977
ISBN-10: 0692886974

Published by Av Lit Press
Contact the author at
www.harrisonjones.org

Dedication

In Memory of
Mary Kay Hardin

In Memory of
Captain Scott Klopfenstein

Acknowledgements

This project is only possible because the following passengers and crew, who were aboard Rocky Mountain Airways Flight 217, were willing to give so generously of their time and effort to revisit and retell the experience. It is truly an honor to know them, and I am privileged beyond words to write their story. My most sincere gratitude to: Vern Bell, First Officer Gary Coleman, Matt Kotts, Jeff Mercer, Luann Mercer, Jon Pratt, Margie Kotts Roosli, and Maureen Redmond Smith. You all have my deep respect and utmost admiration.

Heroes never consider themselves heroes. That definition and title is left for others to assign. I am thankful for the following mission-oriented rescue personnel who put their personal safety in jeopardy to battle a blizzard and overcome every challenge in order to save lives. They have my undying gratitude for allowing me to put their story on a page for others to appreciate. They will always be heroes in my estimation. Thank you: Dan Alsum, Jerry Alsum, Jim Alsum, Harry Blakeman, Doctor Larry Bookman, Jimmy Cure and Jack Donner of the Colorado State Patrol, Sonny Elgin, Rick Hopp, Dave Lindow, Don Niekerk, Steve Poulson, and Bob Werner. I am also grateful for the many other men and women who unselfishly volunteered to assist in the rescue, but I unfortunately did not have the opportunity to interview.

There are so many other people who contributed their thoughts and perspective and allowed me to invade their privacy with intrusive questions in order to complete the story. These include Patty Bell, Manager of Reservations-Sales-and Service for Rocky Mountain Airways; Betty Berger, for educating me on Civil Air Patrol protocol; Captain Dave Boles at RMA for technical advice on the Twin Otter; Bill and Don Coleman who were there for their brother then and now; Debi Coleman, RMA flight attendant, for helping me contact folks to interview; Kelly Coleman for conceiving this project and introducing me to her father; Captain John Gottsleben for insight into the RMA operation; Rod Hanna for climbing a mountain to take amazing rescue photos and sharing them with the world; Dennis Heap, Vice President of Rocky Mountain Airways, for historical documentation at RMA and of Flight 217; Jane Klopfenstein Oates and Virginia Klopfenstein for helping me know more about Captain Scott Klopfenstein; Kathy McKay at the Jackson County Library for research; Ed O'Brien for sharing research, historical data and insight; fellow aviator Ron Plunkett for braving a blizzard to care for a friend and sharing that story; Susan Shoemaker, RMA station agent at Steamboat; and friend, author, and artist Richard Smith for editing and providing illustration. Lastly, I am most fortunate to have the expertise and patience of my editor, Kim Broome. Along with the manuscript, I provided her with compelling evidence that it would be much easier to teach a writer to fly than to teach a pilot to punctuate.

Passenger and Crew Manifest
Rocky Mountain Airways Flight 217
December 4, 1978

Ms. Margie Kotts and infant
Mr. Manfred Bolle
Mr. J. Garbina
Mr. D Brooks
Ms. C Vittone
MS. Luann Stubert
Mr. Jeff Mercer
Mr. John Butts
Mr. Jon Pratt
S. Chanoski
T. Chanoski
N. Chanoski
Mr. Vernon Bell
Ms. Catherine Williams
Ms. Mary Kay Hardin
Ms. Maureen Redmond
Mr. David Erb
Mr. Bob Frolik
Mr. Roger Wobbe

Captain Scott Alan Klopfenstein
First Officer Gary Richard Coleman

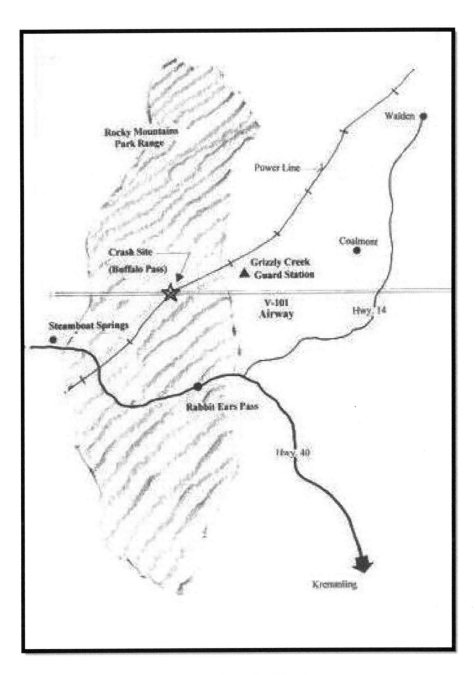

Illustration by Richard Smith

Chapter 1

Flight 216 was late. Not an unusual turn of events for the winter of 1978 in Colorado. The departure from Denver had been delayed, and now strong headwinds were restricting the progress to Steamboat Springs. Captain Scott Klopfenstein and First Officer Gary Coleman prepared for the descent and approach and waited to clear the mountains east of Steamboat. The mountain range was not only an obstacle to navigation—it was also significant for several other reasons. On the west side of the range, the famous Steamboat Ski Resort could be found, and that would eventually be the destination for most of the passengers aboard Flight 216. The east side of the range constituted the Routt National Forest and nothing but wilderness. The ridge line at the top of the range not only divided ski slopes from the wilderness, it also divided the United States of America. The squiggly line on a map represented the Continental Divide.

The aircraft's distance measuring equipment (DME) was not operating to give the pilots a mileage readout to Steamboat making it necessary for them to cross reference two navigation stations to calculate when they would be beyond the mountain and it would be safe to descend. The DME was not required for the flight, but nonetheless very useful in that it would normally display an accurate mileage readout to any navigation station within 200 miles. The Denver Air Traffic Control Center did not provide radar service at the lower altitudes in the Steamboat area, although radio communications were usually good. Despite the strong headwinds and cloud cover, the flight was smooth with surprisingly little turbulence.

When Air Traffic Control cleared Flight 216 to descend, First Officer Coleman read the clearance back and glanced out the cockpit window to inspect the wing and propeller on the right side of the aircraft. Satisfied there was no ice accumulation, he continued to monitor the instruments and review the approach procedure for Steamboat Springs. The weather at the airport was reported as overcast at 2000 feet above the ground and six-miles visibility with light winds—well above the minimums for landing. The temperature hovered in the twenties, and although snow was always a possibility in December, none was reported now. Scott and Gary briefly discussed the familiar approach procedure and agreed the weather was not a problem.

With any luck, they would be able to turn the aircraft around quickly and head back to Denver to complete a long day of flying. Both crewmembers had reported for duty at 12:30 in the afternoon, and now with sunset, they protected their night vision by keeping the cockpit lights to a dim glow.

The flight deck is usually a busy place filled with radio chatter and the continuous banter between pilots. However, there are unspoken traditions when all unnecessary conversation ceases and silence prevails. The view from the cockpit as the big orange ball gradually fades below a distant horizon is one of those times. Only a privileged few have the opportunity to watch the magic of the earth's shadow approach from the east as another day becomes history never to be repeated. To speak unnecessarily would be to identify yourself as a novice and a rookie.

Now that the sunglasses had been tucked away in their flight bag, they slowly sank into the clouds and the runway lights at Steamboat would be a welcome sight when they descended beneath the overcast. Even with a quick turnaround, they would be fortunate to finish their duty day by 8:30. They had been forced to abort the first flight of the day and return to Denver because of the strong westerly headwinds. Every passenger seat would be occupied on the return flight and they would enjoy the advantage of a tailwind.

*****

The passenger terminal at Steamboat Springs consisted of one large room with random seating for customers awaiting arriving and departing flights. Rocky Mountain Airways Flight 217 was scheduled to depart at 4:45 p.m. It was now after six, and the inbound flight was nowhere in sight. Some of the paying customers were voicing their frustration and expressing their displeasure with the airline. Others were accustomed to Colorado weather and the disruption it often caused for most activities—including airline flights. Whether they waited patiently or otherwise—the terminal was their temporary crucible. They were a diverse group.

A young mother cared for her eight-month old son—and waited.

Three young ladies, who worked for the Forest Service, talked about their upcoming training class in Denver—and waited.

A young couple, engaged to be married, discussed their wedding plans—and waited.

A twenty-year old man, on a business trip for his employer, was not intimidated by the challenge of delay—and waited.

A retired military officer was well versed in schedules gone awry—and waited.

A nineteen-year old man from Lakewood, near Denver, was returning home—and waited.

They all waited with one thing in common—the desire to fly to Denver and points beyond—a final destination and an end to the waiting.

The announcement that Flight 216 was arriving was met with relief and anticipation. Passengers near the terminal's window could see the aircraft's landing lights in the distance. Those who chose not to watch the approach soon heard the sound of the turbo-prop engines, first as they were reversed to slow the airplane on the runway, and then again as they idled toward the terminal.

Magically, ramp personnel appeared and prepared to guide the aircraft to its parking spot and begin the process of unloading bags and refueling the airplane for departure. It was a well-choreographed process, and everyone knew their part and played it well. As the engines spun down, heavy chocks were placed fore and aft of the nose wheel, baggage carts were moved into place, doors were opened, the fuel truck rolled up, and passengers were greeted with a smile as they came down the steps and were directed to the terminal door.

The Steamboat ground crew was smooth, and no one noticed how many tasks were accomplished within minutes—just another routine flight turnaround.

Photo courtesy of Rocky Mountain Airways

The de Havilland DHC-6 Twin Otter was a twin engine turbo prop designed to operate into small airports with short runways. Even in the thin air of the Colorado high country, the combination of the powerful engines and the thick wings made it possible to safely operate with barely a half mile of runway. The Twin Otter was classified as a STOL aircraft (Short Takeoff and Landing). The wings were designed for high lift rather than speed. In addition to the nineteen passenger seats, the "Twotter", as it was affectionately known to Rocky Mountain Airways employees, featured a cargo compartment aft of the passenger cabin, a smaller bag bin in the nose of the aircraft, and a detachable cargo pod underneath the fuselage. The belly pod was convenient for transporting passengers' snow skis when they visited the winter resorts and ski slopes near Steamboat Springs.

Rocky Mountain Airways operated as a regional airline and thus was bound to less stringent regulations than the major carriers operating larger aircraft. For example, with only nineteen passenger seats, the Twin Otter did not require a flight attendant on board. The aircraft did not have a cockpit door, and the passengers could clearly see the pilots as they performed their duties. The flight deck crew earned their pay the old fashioned way due to the fact that the airplane was not equipped with an autopilot. They were known in the business as stick and rudder guys, who were more proficient at hand flying than most, due to the necessity of constant practice.

Dennis Heap, a Steamboat Springs resident, served as Vice President of Rocky Mountain Airways and describes how the airline was founded and when the Steamboat Springs station was opened.

"The airline was the brainchild of our founder, Gordon Autry. Gordon was a brilliant visionary with a pioneering spirit and the magic that made a complex system work. Most importantly, he was quick to give credit to the RMA employees for the airline's success and growth. RMA employees were highly trained professionals. They displayed their dedication to Gordon's pioneering spirit and followed his lead of personal accountability and a tireless work ethic. We were a close knit family and the employees understood that success or failure was up to them.

"In the fall of 1971, we began preparations for Steamboat service with the Twin Otter. We installed a navigation beacon in the valley southeast of town and constructed the passenger terminal at the airport. The current airport operator had all the property locked up and was not willing to work with us, so Gordon convinced the Routt County Commissioners to lease the dirt crosswind runway to us. We ordered a modular building for the terminal and drilled a well for potable water—installing a holding tank for sewerage. The well-drillers hit brackish looking water that smelled like sulfur and could only be used for hand washing and flushing.

"Winter set in before the ramp and parking lot could be paved, but nevertheless, we began flights on January 1, 1972. Steamboat was our third ski destination. The end of winter brought the *mud season* and RMA personnel had new challenges. The Twin Otter could taxi through the mud to the terminal, but passengers were not eager to wade through the mud to get into the building. The solution was the construction of wooden boardwalks to get customers to the terminal then part way to the parking lot. It was not uncommon for the station manager to use his Jeep to pull passenger vehicles to the highway so they could begin their trip to town. After the passengers were gone, the mud in the terminal was cleaned with a snow shovel. In the summer of 1972, the paving was completed and our passengers were served with a modern and convenient terminal. We also gained access to the paved runway and our Steamboat operation finally met our expectations.

"Rocky Mountain's most significant contributions to Colorado aviation was the development of all-weather, day-night service to mountain airports by making full use of STOL technology. The program required a unique aircraft and unique ground-based navigational aids. RMA purchased the de Havilland Twin Otter and the de Havilland Dash-7. Both aircraft were selected for their unique qualities as descendants of bush country airplanes designed to operate off short landing strips in geographically confined areas.

"RMA struggled with baggage because neither the Twin Otter nor the Dash-7 had bag compartments large enough to meet the demands of skiers. We flew the Otter with a nineteen passenger capacity and when we were full with ski passengers, the luggage was too much for the baggage compartment. We loaded skis under the cabin seats, which gave the passengers an up close and personal experience with the skis as they had to rest their feet on them. A significant solution was the development of ski pods, which were fitted to the belly of the Otters. RMA received FAA approval to modify the airplane in the form of a supplemental type certificate, which approved the modification and its effect on the original design and performance of the airplane.

"A company owned microwave landing system (MLS) was installed at Steamboat in 1973. The system was developed for military use in Southeast Asia to permit precision landing approaches in terrain and weather conditions that would distort conventional radio beam Instrument Landing Systems (ILS). In addition, RMA installed electronic aids including strobe lights, obstruction lights, visual approach slope indicator lights (VASI), and medium-intensity runway lights. We also established a Supplementary Aviation Weather Reporting Station (SAWRS) in Steamboat, which was approved by the National Weather Service.

"RMA carried over a million people to the ski areas in nineteen passenger Twin Otters. The aircraft was not pressurized, and passengers often imitated the two-man crew by removing the reusable oxygen mask and putting the tube in their mouth."

Photo Courtesy of Rocky Mountain Airways

First Officer Coleman remembers, "Flight 216, from Denver to Steamboat, was Scott's leg and he was flying the airplane. The terminal weather reports we received from Routt County (Steamboat) were satisfactory, and we planned an ADF (a low frequency radio navigation beacon, located near the air field) instrument approach. Our DME (Distance Measuring Equipment) was out so we didn't have an accurate distance or ground speed readout from the Hayden VOR nav station. I cross referenced the Kremmling VOR in order to determine our distance from Steamboat and calculate when it would be safe to descend. The ride was smooth and the descent, approach, and landing were all routine, except we did pick up a light to moderate coating of rime ice on the approach. We activated the de-ice system, and it cleared the protected surfaces without a problem. After landing, we taxied to the terminal, shut down, and did the paperwork. The station agent wanted to begin the boarding process as soon as possible."

First Officer Coleman went through the familiar routine and shut down the engines. With the checklist complete, and the luxury of relative silence in the cockpit, both pilots turned their attention to the departure as they listened to the chatter of passengers gathering their belongings and moving aft to the exit door on the left side of the aircraft.

Flight 216 became history as the block times were recorded and the aircraft logbook entries were completed. Both pilots were surprised that the block time for Flight 216 was almost two hours and calculated that they had experienced at least a seventy knot headwind. The normal cruise speed for the Otter was 150 knots, and the wind had reduced the groundspeed to about eighty. They discussed the possibility that the company might cancel the Denver flight due to the winds and the possibility of icing conditions, and they were not opposed to a night at the hotel in Steamboat. However, Rocky Mountain Airways Flight 217 to Denver was now posted and would become active in the FAA Air Traffic Control system as soon as the flight plan was filed.

Both pilots were experienced and knew their duties well. Captain Scott Klopfenstein was twenty-nine years old and held the Airline Transport Pilot license for both single and multi-engine aircraft. The ATP is the highest pilot rating that can be obtained. He also held a special type rating for the de Havilland DHC-6 Twin Otter. Scott had accumulated over 7000 hours total flying time and had recently passed his annual First Class Medical Exam as well as his FAA proficiency check ride in the airplane. He was currently undergoing the interview process with American Airlines and hoped to soon be flying for the major carrier.

First Officer Gary Coleman was thirty-four years old and more qualified than most copilots. Gary also held the Airline Transport Pilot license for single and multi-engine aircraft, even though it wasn't required of first officers. The ATP is sometimes referred to as the PhD of aviation. In addition, he was also licensed as a Certified Flight Instructor and was well experienced in teaching both private and commercial flying. He also had worked as an aircraft mechanic while learning to fly and had accumulated almost 4000 hours of flying time. He had recently passed his First Class Medical Exam required by the FAA. Both pilots were single and devoted to their flying career.

With their cockpit duties complete, the two pilots walked aft through the empty cabin. The narrow aisle separated a row of double seats on the right side of the aircraft and a single row on the left. An additional three seats were attached to the aft bulkhead that separated the passenger cabin from the baggage compartment. After being confined to the seat in the cramped cockpit for several hours, both men welcomed the opportunity to stretch their legs. When they reached the rear of the cabin, they walked down the steps, which were built into the passenger entrance door, and were greeted by the chill of the Colorado night.

Scott headed to the terminal and the telephone to call the company dispatcher in Denver in order to discuss the weather for the return flight, the required fuel load, the weight and balance numbers, and the route of flight. Gary remained with the aircraft and began his preflight inspection. The sun was well below the horizon, and the evening was damp with the temperature reported at twenty-five degrees Fahrenheit. Gary might have been uncomfortable were it not for his wool uniform pants and black wool uniform sweater. His mother had worried that the cockpit would be cold at the higher altitudes and had bought the items for him to replace the standard polyester uniform. As usual, his mom was correct and he was grateful.

As he began to walk around the aircraft, he was not surprised to find areas of ice accumulation coating the unprotected areas of the fuselage and wings since they had encountered a brief period of icing conditions during the approach. It was not an unusual occurrence since, as with almost all aircraft, only the leading edge of the wings, the tail, and the engines were equipped with de-ice systems. The windshield was also electrically heated to prevent ice from forming and restricting forward visibility. His discovery simply meant that he would have to employ the company approved method for ice removal. The rudimentary procedure entailed using a broom handle to tap the ice and crack it off the metal surfaces. Simple, but effective.

Ice accumulation is a hazard to flight for two reasons. First, it adds unnecessary weight to the airplane which inhibits the maximum speed and altitude. Secondly, and sometimes more importantly, it changes the shape of the wings and decreases the ability to create lift. The Twin Otter came equipped with a de-ice system designed to protect the critical surfaces of the airplane.

Gary later recounted, "I finished the paperwork and made sure we were refueled and the passenger oxygen system was topped off, then started the walk around. The ramp rats (ground personnel) and I knocked off the ice on the unprotected surfaces and when the walk around was complete, I went inside to talk to Scott about the ice and the wind at altitude. He had finished the call to dispatch, so I didn't hear the conversation. Safety was always the first priority, but I got the impression there may have been a discussion about the passengers waiting all day and the fact that the airplane was needed in Denver for subsequent flights."

Nonetheless, the two pilots discussed the weather and the forecast of possible icing conditions. The return flight would be retracing the route they had just flown, and the only ice they had encountered on the inbound flight was on the approach into Steamboat.

Gary said, "We went out to check on the Otter and were surprised to see the moon and stars as the weather seemed to be improving. The wind was calm, and it appeared to be clear to the west toward Hayden. Since our departure started to the west to the Hayden VOR, and then a course reversal to intercept the airway headed eastbound, our groundspeed would be slower than normal during the climb, and we should have no trouble reaching 10,000 feet before turning east toward the mountains."

Chapter 2

It had already been a long day for passenger Jeff Mercer and his bride to be. Jeff and Luann had been high school sweethearts, and now they were on their way to Ocala, Florida where they were to be married. Jeff's family in Florida awaited their arrival and looked forward to celebrating the upcoming wedding.

Jeff said, "We were scheduled to depart from Hayden, Colorado Airport in route to Denver and a final connecting flight to Orlando where we would meet relatives. We drove from Savery, Wyoming to Hayden where we waited for our flight. Due to snowy weather, the Hayden Airport canceled all flights. We then drove from Hayden to the Steamboat Springs Airport in hopes of catching a flight to Denver in order to connect to Orlando. The entire day was snowy—snow on the ground and cold temperatures."

After arriving at Steamboat, the couple found that two seats were available on Rocky Mountain Airways Flight 217 to Denver. The flight was scheduled to depart at 4:45 p.m. and they checked two large suitcases containing their personal belongings along with the wedding invitations. The invitations were carefully packed among the warm weather clothes for Florida. Luann decided to keep her wedding dress with her as a carry on item. Protected by a plastic garment bag, she did not want to chance it being soiled or damaged.

Jeff remembered, "The delays were long and the Steamboat Springs airport was waiting for conditions to improve in order to begin outbound flights. We waited, watched, and talked to each other as well as others who were waiting to fly out. Luann was very concerned about the weather conditions. It was her first flight, and I concluded that her concerns were 'first flight' nerves. Some of the people in the airport had decided to rent a car and drive to Denver. They asked if we would like to join them, but my feeling at the time was it would be safer to wait for a flight out rather than drive in the snowy conditions."

After more waiting, the inbound flight finally arrived and the boarding process began. With a light mist falling, they walked across the ramp and climbed the few steps onto the airplane. Luann carefully held to the wedding dress.

Jeff said, "Luann was concerned once again when we saw airport workers using brooms to remove snow and ice from the aircraft and the wings. We were seated together on the right side of the cabin near the front."

*****

Passenger Maureen Redmond recalls, "I was working for the Agriculture Department Forest Service, and three of us were going to Denver for a training session. I had forgotten about it until just the day before. I did not want to go at all. I was working on a quilt for my boyfriend for Christmas and was almost done, and I absolutely hated to drive over Rabbit Ears Pass in the winter. The personnel officer told me we could fly, and it was just a one-day training, so…

"We all three had packed and each of us brought our one bag to the office that morning. I think we were to leave around noon. I did my usual work in the morning and a co-worker was going to drive us to the airport. The weather was terrible—windy, snowy, damp, and cold. When we went to the car, the doors were frozen closed by a quarter inch of ice. We had to use the ice scraper to chip them open. However, off we went to the airport, feeling happy that we were not driving over Rabbit Ears Pass on the terrible roads. The terminal was crowded because no flights had been able to come in all day, so no one was able to leave. Only the people with the most pressing need to get out of town were still waiting.

"Some people were frustrated and angry, but I was feeling uneasy and just as glad to sit and wait. A few times we discussed among ourselves if we should just cancel out. The Agriculture Department had to pay for the training we were assigned to attend, so we felt obligated to wait. I think if I had my own car at the airport, I would have just called it and left.

"As the hours went by, I felt more and more uneasy. I had flown Rocky Mountain Airways before and enjoyed the flights. The weather was just so terrible and it was a good night to stay home, but I waited with the other two ladies. After the plane came in from Denver, I saw people chipping ice off the airplane with broom handles. I think the pilots were helping, and they seemed relaxed and unconcerned. When I saw that ice, I got a bad feeling and was very anxious.

"When we boarded the flight, my two friends wouldn't let me sit with them in the very back because they said I was making them nervous, so I took an aisle seat on the right side of the plane under the wing. Next to me, at the window, was a mom with an eight-month old baby, Margie and Matthew Kotts. She said not to worry, she flew back and forth all the time in all kinds of weather."

*****

Twenty-year old Jon Pratt was the newest employee in the engineering department of Energy Fuels Coal Mine near Steamboat Springs. Accomplished beyond his years, Jon had earned the title of Eagle Scout under the tutelage of his father. This was no small task considering the arduous requirements were met in the mountainous terrain and winter weather of Colorado. When asked, Jon was quick to credit his Scoutmaster dad for teaching him skiing, hiking, rock climbing, first aid, and camping skills. Digging a snow cave, and sleeping in it overnight, was little challenge for an Eagle Scout.

Jon said, "As the youngest and newest employee in the office, I was asked to do lots of special task. When I arrived on December the fourth, my boss asked me to fly up to Gillette, Wyoming to pick up a new truck and drive it down to the mine. I headed home and packed for what can be a long lonely drive across the plains of Wyoming with very few towns. Following the Boy Scout motto of 'Be Prepared,' I packed for the worst conditions in mind. I may have overdone it a bit, but I knew running a truck into the ditch on 400 miles of two lane roads that were snow packed, with wind-blown whiteouts, was a real possibility.

"In one bag, I loaded a mountain parka, gloves, winter hat, and a down sleeping bag just in case I wound up sleeping in the truck. In the other bag was a change of clothes, a small camping stove, and a pot to heat and melt snow for water. Of course, in those days, you could carry a propane stove onto a commercial plane along with the knife which I always carried in my pocket.

"I headed to the airport and was scheduled on an early afternoon flight. When that flight was canceled, I called the office and asked what I should do. They said I should just stay put and wait to see if I could get out later and still make it to Gillette or just stay in Denver overnight. This was my first business trip ever, and at twenty years old, I was not about to spend money I might not be reimbursed for. I remember a lot of people in and out and on the pay phone trying to rearrange plans as flights continued to be canceled. One of the passengers waiting was Steamboat legend 'Billy the Kid.'"

Billy Kidd was a famous Olympic skier and had won numerous medals for the United States. He now lived in Steamboat and served as an ambassador for the ski resort industry. He was easily recognizable by the Stetson cowboy hat he always wore.

"I thought it might be interesting to be on the same flight with a celebrity. Later in the afternoon, Billy gave up and decided to drive to Denver. I waited patiently with no serious agenda or appointment to make. I was interested in an attractive young woman who I tried to strike up a conversation with, but as the saying goes, 'I struck out.'"

Photo Courtesy of Rocky Mountain Airways

"When Flight 216 finally arrived, I watched it taxi in and deplane. When they began preparing it for departure, I noticed the

14

Miracle on Buffalo Pass

broom handle de-icing technique with interest. I assumed the pilots knew what they were doing. I saw one of my bags loaded in the cargo hold behind the passenger door and the other in the nose of the plane.

"After waiting most of the afternoon, we finally walked across the tarmac to board the plane, and I noticed it was only slightly snowing after a day of fairly steady snowfall. I thought that meant an easy flight into Denver. As I came up the steps, there was the young woman I had tried to talk with earlier, and I took the opportunity to claim the empty seat next to her right by the door. I was empty handed, as were most people, with almost no room for carry-ons in a plane I could not fully stand up in."

*****

Lieutenant Colonel Roger Wobbe was retired from the United States Air Force. The World War II veteran had enjoyed a distinguished aviation career and was not particularly concerned about the flight to Denver. He had flown in many types of aircraft and all kinds of weather and waited patiently for the boarding process to begin. He found a seat near the front of the passenger cabin for the forty-five-minute flight to Denver.

*****

Nineteen-year old Vern Bell was returning to Denver after delivering a vehicle to Steamboat Springs for his boss. Vern said, "I delivered the truck to one of the mines near Steamboat and then caught a ride to the airport for the flight home. As I recall, the drive from Denver had been uneventful, and I had no real issues with the roads. However, I remember the snow became heavier later in the day while I waited at the airport.

"Although it was December, I was lightly dressed since it was just a day trip, and I wasn't going skiing. I was wearing tennis shoes, jeans, a shirt, and a mid-weight flight jacket I had purchased at a military surplus store. The flight was delayed, and all I could do was wait with the other passengers and wonder what time I would get home.

15

"Oddly enough, since I rarely flew, I found myself looking around at the other people waiting and thinking to myself, *what would happen, and how would these people react, if we were in a plane crash?* I had recently read a story in *Reader's Digest* about a plane crash, and I guess that had me thinking of the possibilities. I was glad to see the inbound flight arrive and boarding the airplane was uneventful."

*****

With the ice accumulation removed, and the airplane deemed airworthy, the two pilots returned to the cockpit to prepare for departure. The station agent confirmed that he had refueled the tanks with the requested fuel load of 1200 pounds of jet fuel and that he had also refilled the passenger oxygen system. The Twin Otter was not a pressurized aircraft, and it was necessary to provide supplemental oxygen for each passenger when the flight exceeded 10,000 feet. An oxygen mask was provided at each seat, and the mask was connected to the ship's oxygen supply through a clear plastic tube. The flight plan to Denver called for a cruise altitude of 17,000 feet—well above the minimum to safely fly above the mountains along the route, and also an altitude that would provide the most comfortable ride for the passengers. The agent also verified that the passenger cabin would be fully occupied with nineteen adults and one infant in his mom's lap and confirmed the cargo and baggage weights were accurate. The pilots quickly did the math and carefully calculated the takeoff weight to be 12,017 pounds and within limits for normal aircraft performance.

The agent wished them a good flight and left to button up the door. He then walked forward of the aircraft, where he was visible to the cockpit, and raised both arms above his head with clinched fist, reminding the captain to set the brakes. Scott returned the signal by showing clinched fist and verifying the parking brakes were set. The agent pointed to the right engine and then raised his right arm and spun his finger in a circle to indicate that the area was clear and the engine could be started. Scott flipped the aircraft's red rotating beacon on to alert everyone in the area that the engine was about to spin and engaged the starter. The low whine of the engine became louder as the

16

RPM increased and became a steady roar when the fuel lever was moved to the on position. Gary noted the time on the instrument panel clock and wrote the block out time on his pad next to the ATC clearance.

Gary said, "Engine start and taxi out were uneventful as was the engine run up. We gave extra attention to testing the de-ice boot cycle, the heated props, and the windshield heat. We checked the pitot heat (airspeed sensors on the exterior of the cockpit) carefully."

The before takeoff checklist called for setting both altimeters to the current reported barometric pressure, and they checked to see that both instruments indicated the field elevation of 6879 feet above sea level. An aircraft altimeter is basically a barometer, and as the barometric pressure decreases (as in a climb), the instrument indicates the increase in altitude. The accuracy of the altimeter is dependent on setting the known local barometric pressure and checking that it reads the known elevation.

When the weather is reported on the local TV news, everyone ignores the barometric pressure, but to a pilot, it is very significant. A variation of .01 inches of mercury results in a change of ten feet on the altimeter. Once the aircraft departs the local area, the pilots depend on ATC to keep them updated on altimeter settings along the route of flight. ATC depends on accurate weather reporting stations in order to pass that information to the cockpit. When flying through an area of low barometric pressure, the aircraft will be lower than the altimeter indicates if uncorrected. The correct setting will result in feet above sea level and also keep two aircraft safely separated vertically if both have the correct setting applied.

The airport at Steamboat Springs was an 'uncontrolled airport' which simply meant it did not have a control tower. Typically, small airports in the United States do not have a tower, and pilots are responsible for separating themselves from other traffic until they contact the air traffic control center once they are airborne. After carefully scanning the traffic pattern to make sure no other aircraft were in the area, Scott taxied onto the runway and lined up with 3310 feet of pavement ahead of them. He flipped the landing lights on and said, "You have the airplane, Gary."

Both pilots checked that their seat belts were snug. The flight deck seats did not feature a shoulder harness or a crotch strap—only lap belts. Gary jotted down the takeoff time at 6:55 p.m. before reaching up to the overhead panel and pushing the throttles forward to begin the takeoff roll.

Gary continued, "It was my leg to Denver and the Otter was a treat to fly. It was somewhat similar to the small aircraft both Scotty and I had done our early teething on. Takeoff and climb were uneventful and when we reached 10,000 feet, we broke out our oxygen mask and put them on. We turned east, joined the airway, and began our climb to 17,000 feet. As we passed the glow of Steamboat below and to our right, we were climbing through 11,000 feet.

"The lights of the city disappeared and our climb rate slowed. We were in and out of the clouds and probably approaching the leeward side of Buffalo Pass. The DME was still inoperative, but our ground speed was incredible according to the cross reference of Kremmling VOR.

"I was flying and Scott was on the radio and monitoring engine power settings. The rate of climb continued to decrease as we neared 11,500 feet. Our MEA (minimum en-route altitude) would be 13,000 feet as we continued on the airway. I nursed the rate of climb until we entered a cloud bank at about 12,500 feet near the mountain ridge at Buffalo Pass. We encountered some icing, but the deicing equipment was removing it from the protected areas, including the wings, the props and the windshield with no problem."

Experienced pilots perform routine tasks and maneuvers instinctively. Normal procedures are accomplished by establishing good habit patterns that are repeated consistently thousands of times. With repetition comes confidence and many pilots can sit in the cockpit with their eyes closed and correctly identify hundreds of switches and controls just by touch.

The speed of an airplane demands that the pilot's attention is focused far ahead both in time and space. Establishing good habit patterns for routine checklist and procedures frees the mind to multi-task and concentrate on more important things.

However, when the normal habit pattern doesn't produce the normal result, it is immediately and abundantly clear to the pilot, and intuitively he or she will scan the here and now to find out why.

Scott and Gary both knew the Otter should be climbing at a rate of a thousand feet per minute and it was not. They had accounted for the icing conditions in their preflight planning and knew that was not the only factor in the aircraft's decreased performance.

Gary continued, "When we finally reached 13,000 feet, the aircraft would not climb higher. Scott inched the power up, but it just wouldn't climb. We traded duties a couple of times thinking one of us might be better than the other. Scotty said, 'Can you make this pig fly?'"

It was later discovered that an un-forecast and un-reported mountain wave had developed over the ridge at Buffalo Pass due to the strong westerly winds aloft. The mountain of air spilling over the ridge created tremendous downdrafts even though it created little turbulence—attributed to the fact that the summit was smooth and rounded. The pilots had no way of knowing the aircraft's climb performance was being diminished by the descending air mass surrounding them.

Gary said, "Our next altitude crossing restriction was at Kater intersection (a waypoint on the airway, east of Buffalo Pass) and our MOCA (minimum obstruction clearance altitude) at that point would be 16,000 feet. With the strong tailwind and the slow rate of climb, that was just not going to happen. We were approaching way too fast to be able to make this altitude and were experiencing downdrafts that did not seem to be diminishing. Now, we were at 13,000 feet and the aircraft refused to climb higher even though Scott continued to inch the throttles up to maintain maximum power. Raising the nose only resulted in lower airspeed with no corresponding climb."

The pilots were now faced with a dilemma. Continuing east, toward the higher peaks of the Front Range, was not an option unless they could climb. The engines seemed to be operating fine and producing plenty of power, and the icing condition appeared to be minimal, but the airplane just would not climb.

Gary said, "We both knew that the Front Range of the Rocky Mountains varied from 13,200 to 14,280 feet and continuing was just not safe. Our present position was over the high plain of North Park— a mostly level region with an elevation of about 8000 feet. We briefly considered trying to escape to the north or south, but we would still have mountains to contend with as well as off-route weather conditions. We were at 13,000 feet, which was a safe altitude for our position, and not descending so the decision was made to divert back to Steamboat."

Pilots always have a contingency plan in the back of their mind in case of an emergency. They are always aware of the nearest suitable airport if it becomes necessary to make an immediate landing. The contingency plan for the early portion of Flight 217 was to return to Steamboat. There were two other airports in the area—one at Kremmling and the other at Walden. A 12,000-foot mountain range eliminated Kremmling as an option, and if they descended toward Walden, there was no guarantee they would be able to see the runway with the low visibility and no assurance they would be able to climb back to altitude. They were more familiar with the airport at Steamboat, and they knew the weather had been basically clear, with light winds, just twenty minutes earlier. You can't call time out in an airplane, and there is no pause button. You can't pull to the side of the road and analyze a problem. Decisions have to be made, and you don't have long to think about it.

At 7:14 Flight 217 reported to Denver, "We're going to have to return to Steamboat."

The Denver controller replied, "Rocky Mountain 217, what's your position now?"

"We're on the…340 radial of Kremmling, on the north side…"

"Roger, Rocky Mountain 217, you're cleared to Steamboat to cruise 17,000."

The response from 217 was garbled. A cruise clearance in the vernacular of aviation means the altitude limit is 17,000, but you are cleared to descend at your discretion.

Gary explained, "As Scotty was calling Denver Center to change our flight plan, I began the turn. As an airplane makes a turn, some vertical lift is lost. At a normal airspeed this lessening of lift is not noticed, but at our low speed, we had no choice but to descend to maintain a safe margin above stall. This slight descent was only a hundred feet or so and it put us into more icing, but it was not significant."

At 7:15 the controller said, "Rocky Mountain 217, proceed direct to Steamboat at your discretion and let me know…what's your altitude now?"

Flight 217 replied, "13,000."

The Denver controller then transmitted, "Rocky Mountain 217, roger, change to advisory frequency is approved, report your cancellation or ground time on this frequency or through dispatch."

No reply was recorded from Flight 217.

Gary described the return to Steamboat, "After we turned back, having lost a bit of altitude in the turn, we rejoined the airway and were in and out of the clouds. There were periods when we were in the clear and moonlight illuminated the clouds…which reinforced the decision to return to Steamboat. We had apparently flown over the worst of the icing while flying east. We popped out of the clouds for a short period, and I glanced up to see what appeared to be a black cloud with white stripes sloping down to the east. We were going to enter the top of that cloud without any choice. I don't remember what I said, but Scotty looked up from his radio duties and said, 'Oh shit…my airplane!'

"The icing in that cloud was so severe that the airplane felt as though it slowed down. It probably did. One of the sensory inputs pilots use is *seat of your pants*. When you move forward in the seat, the airplane has slowed down. Conversely, when you move back in the seat, the airplane has accelerated. I moved forward! In hindsight, the clouds sloping down to the east were probably a visual indication of the mountain wave which was not allowing us to climb."

When strong winds lift a mass of moisture-laden air up a mountain slope, the atmosphere is cooled as the altitude increases, and the moisture condenses to become visible in the form of a cloud. In the case of a mountain wave, the cloud that forms at the crest is often known as a lenticular cloud. It usually appears as a dome or cap at the summit. Pilots are well aware of the danger a lenticular cloud creates, both in terms of icing and turbulence as well as downdrafts. Scott and Gary were only afforded a brief view of the ominous cloud in the windshield and it didn't matter. They could not climb and they could not turn without sacrificing precious altitude. They were committed.

Gary described the experience, "The icing was so heavy that it formed aft of the de-ice boots, behind the leading edge of the wing, as well as on the boots themselves. When the pneumatic boots expanded and popped the leading edge ice off, it left a ridge of ice behind the boots, further degrading the lift of our fat Otter wings. In addition, every unprotected surface had a good coating of ice, increasing our gross weight.

"We switched the navigation radios so Scotty was now flying the airway back to Hayden, and I was cross referencing the radials off Kremmling. I had the radial dialed in that would let us know when we were beyond Buffalo Pass and could start a descent."

At 7:17, the controller called the station agent at Steamboat Springs on the telephone and told him that 217 was returning to Steamboat. According to the agent, about five minutes later Flight 217 radioed him that it was returning because of heavy icing and recommended that other flights not attempt to fly into Steamboat Springs.

At 7:19 the Denver controller asked, "Rocky Mountain 217, you still on frequency?"

Flight 217 replied, "Yes, still here."

The controller made two other transmissions to Flight 217 but received unintelligible replies—probably due to ice on the aircraft's radio antennas.

Gary described the situation, "We were doing okay until we approached the leeward slope of Buffalo Pass. The airplane began an 800 to 1000 foot per minute descent that we could not stop without sacrificing airspeed that was already at the edge of a stall. We were maintaining about 90 knots and anything less resulted in a pre-stall buffet. Anything more resulted in a descent. With the headwind, we were barely making progress. Scott called for ten degrees of flaps in an attempt to increase lift and allow us to fly a few knots slower without stalling. I moved the flap handle to ten degrees, and it seemed to help— at least temporarily."

At 7:39, Flight 217 transmitted "…want you to be aware that we're having a little problem here maintaining altitude and proceeding direct Steamboat beacon."

"Roger, what's your position now, Sir?"

At 7:40 Flight 217 replied "We're on Victor 101 crossing the 335 of Kremmling."

The controller then asked, "Rocky Mountain 217, okay Sir, can I give you any assistance?"

Flight 217 replied, "Not now."

Gary said, "The radio calls from center were annoying and distracting, asking for every bit of information, and there was nothing they could do to help. I answered when I could but we were very busy. Without an autopilot, we literally had our hands full. The airplane was not equipped with a radar altimeter to give us a readout on our height above the ground, and we had not received a barometric altimeter correction since takeoff. I was very concerned that we might be lower than the altimeter indicated, but there was absolutely nothing we could do."

Neither of the pilots could have known about the dangerous mountain wave condition that had not been forecast but now existed over Buffalo Pass. Nor could they know that the river of air flowing up the mountain and down the other side was probably lowering the barometric pressure just as air flowing over a wing decreases the pressure on top and creates lift. The descending mass of air was slowly taking the airplane down with it no matter how hard the crew fought or how skilled they were. The laws of aerodynamics are somewhat simple but nonetheless—unforgiving.

Gary said, "About this time, we flew into another patch of severe icing. The heated windscreen was so hot you couldn't touch it, yet it was still partially iced over. Every piece of de-ice equipment was working but could not keep up. With our nose pitched up to hold altitude, we even picked up ice on the bottom of the wing. We were in dense clouds and could not see the end of the wing.

"I had the Kremmling VOR radial set up that would tell us when we cleared the mountain. The needle moved agonizingly slow as it neared center and indicated that we were very close, if not over Buffalo Pass."

Scott said, "I think we've got it made."

At 7:44 the Denver controller received a radio transmission that he believed was from Flight 217. The controller replied four times to the transmission but received no response.

Chapter 3

With Flight 217 loaded with ice and in the grip of a downdraft, Scott and Gary hung the Otter on its props and fought for every foot of altitude and every knot of airspeed as they neared the summit at Buffalo Pass. Without the DME, they could not be sure of their exact position, but every second of forward progress was precious. They were both acutely aware that the situation required total concentration and complete focus. Fear or distraction was not a luxury they could afford. Altitude and airspeed were essential to flight, but most of all they needed time to clear the mountain top. They each called on years of training to provide seconds of flight. After thousands of hours staring at flight instruments, the little round clock in the corner of the panel loomed large and ticked a steady rhythm at sixty beats a minute. It was the one instrument that no amount of skill or talent could control.

Gary said, "I saw what I thought was an incredibly bright blue flash of lightning out of the right cockpit window and felt a jolt. The landing lights were on and mostly reflected nothing but heavy snow. At almost a hundred miles per hour, the falling flakes passed the window horizontally, but then for about a second or two, the ground appeared in the lights, and I knew we had lost the battle."

In the dark, with visibility down to nothing in heavy snow, the pilots could not see the long line of high voltage transmission towers that crossed the summit of Buffalo Pass. The right wing had clipped one of the eighty-foot tall towers and the 230,000-volt power line—causing an electrical short and thus the bright blue flash of light momentarily illuminating the mountain side.

Gary continued, "With the engines already straining at maximum climb power, I instinctively shoved the throttles and prop controls full forward anyway. Straight ahead, I could see a dark area and to the right a white area. Scotty must have noticed the same thing, and I think we both kicked the right rudder to steer toward the white area."

It was later discovered that the dark area the airplane was headed for was an embankment with rocks, and the white area was deep snow. By exercising their last possible bit of control, the survivability of the crash was greatly enhanced. The last tick of the clock occurred at 7:45 p.m. The altimeter finally stopped its maddening descent, and the airspeed went to zero.

The instrument panel somehow maintained electrical power and continued to glow. Scott's uncorrected altimeter indicated 10,615 feet above sea level. The National Transportation and Safety Board would later determine the actual altitude to be 10,530 feet above sea level and just 150 feet below the ridge at Buffalo Pass. Every accident begs the question, "What if?"

What if the headwind had been a few knots less?

What if the aircraft gross weight had been a few hundred pounds less?

What if somehow we could control the tick of a clock?

Without the restraint of a shoulder harness, both pilots were defenseless and impacted the control column and instrument panel. The deceleration force actually broke Scott's pilot seat from its attachment to the floor, and he was launched forward and to the right. His injuries were severe for several reasons, including the fact that he continued to valiantly grip the controls tightly to maneuver the airplane even as the impact force tried to rip them from his hands. Instead of the controls moving the flight surfaces, the flight surfaces were now moving the controls. The captain's arms were broken in several places due to the violent movement of the control column.

Gary said, "When we hit the ground, I was thrown forward and must have blacked out."

The copilot suffered a concussion, internal injuries, numerous lacerations, contusions, and eventually frostbite. His left hand was mangled due to the fact that he was still gripping the throttles when the engines departed the airplane and popped the cables connected to the power controls in the cockpit.

It was later determined that the forward speed of the airplane at impact was only about forty knots. The pilots were maintaining an airspeed of eighty to ninety knots, however the National Transportation and Safety Board later estimated the headwind at the summit to be as much as sixty knots, which reduced the actual speed over the ground. This theory was supported by the fact that the debris field was only about 200 feet from the first impact until the fuselage came to rest. In addition, the pilots were maintaining a nose up attitude, as if in a climb, in order to preserve as much altitude as possible. The climb attitude of the airplane somewhat matched the upslope of the mountain and thus avoided a catastrophic nose first impact.

The right wing had initially clipped a high voltage power line, or transmission tower, or possibly both. Ten feet of the right wing was ripped off at initial contact, and the remainder separated from the fuselage when it slammed to the ground. As the airplane continued sliding forward, the left wing and engine also separated. The left wing flipped upside down and spun around leaving the outboard tip next to the fuselage. Now, there were gaping holes in the passenger cabin where the wings had been attached. The fuselage rolled and finally came to rest on its right side in several feet of snow.

Maureen Redmond was seated next to Margie Kotts and her infant son, and now snow was blowing in through the opening above their seat where the wing had been before. The nose of the airplane, including the forward baggage bin, was destroyed and the cockpit windshield shattered. As the airplane bulldozed forward, snow was scooped in to pack the tight flight deck space. With the airplane now on its right side, Gary was on the bottom and took the brunt of most of the snow being packed into the cockpit—possibly a blessing in disguise. Airplanes do not have air bags as in modern autos, but Gary said, "I may have been the first pilot in history to benefit from a snow bag."

The left side of the cockpit—Scott's side of the flight deck—was ripped open and missing, and now snow and wind filled the void. The wind continued to spill over the summit of Buffalo Pass, and the snow continued to fall.

*****

In scattered areas around northwest Colorado and southern Wyoming, the lights brightened then dimmed and blinked out. Customers, who had paid their power bill on time, began calling to complain. Some called the power company, but many called the sheriff's office. It was soon determined that a circuit breaker which protected the cross country high voltage transmission lines had tripped. After troubleshooting the circuits, the breaker was reset after only a few minutes, and the lights came on and the phone calls stopped.

When contact was lost with Flight 217, the controller in Denver promptly notified his supervisor. The supervisor plugged a headset in and listened as the controller requested other aircraft in the vicinity to try to contact Rocky Mountain 217. When it became apparent that wasn't going to happen, the supervisor initiated the established protocol for such an event, and eventually the U.S Air Force Mission Command Center at Scott Air Force Base, Illinois was alerted.

Authorization came quickly and the notification process began. All aircraft in the vicinity as well as all emergency services, including local law enforcement, in the general area were made aware that Rocky Mountain Airways Flight 217 was probably down. Emergency dispatchers keyed radio mics, radios crackled, and in a few minutes, patrol cars everywhere were on the lookout. Hospitals and medical personnel were informed that they should standby. Local news media, who monitored all police and fire radio frequencies, picked up on the story and assigned reporters and camera crews. They had no idea where to go but began contacting sources and asking questions.

The first response came from an Air Force Reserve C-130 flying high above the weather over the Steamboat area. The air force crew routinely monitored the international emergency frequency of 121.5 and had picked up the wailing sound of an emergency locator transmitter. Rocky Mountain Airways had equipped its Twin Otters with the ELT, and it was designed to automatically begin transmitting an emergency signal when it sensed the G force of an impact. The C-130 was not equipped with the special direction finding equipment necessary to pinpoint the location, but based on the strength of the audio signal, they estimated the source to be near Walden, Colorado. Shortly after that, a Colorado state highway employee, traveling south on State Route Fourteen, reported that he had observed the red and green position lights of a low flying aircraft to his right. He said he was near mile post eleven and north of the intersection with Highway Forty.

The emergency locator transmitter was a fairly recent addition to the aviation industry and deserves a brief review of its history. In the fall of 1972 the political campaign season was well underway and Congressman Hale Boggs (D-LA) had traveled to Alaska where he would attend a fundraiser for Congressman Nick Begich (D-AK). As Majority Leader, Congressman Boggs often campaigned for fellow democrats. The two friends met in Anchorage where they boarded a chartered Cessna-310 twin-engine aircraft operated by Pan Alaska Airways. The company's chief pilot, Don Jonz, was in command of the flight. Congressman Begich's aide, Russell Brown, was also along for the trip.

On October 16, 1972, the flight departed Anchorage on a three hour and thirty-minute VFR (visual flight rules) flight plan to Juneau. Low clouds and fog were forecast for the route of flight, and the airplane disappeared as it approached the Chugach Mountain Range in southeast Alaska. The aircraft and four souls on board have never been seen or heard from since. Conspiracy theories abounded as Hale Boggs had served on the Warren Commission and had not always agreed with the conclusions they drew concerning President Kennedy's assassination. The incident triggered what would be the biggest search in U.S. history at the time. For the next thirty-nine days, forty military and twenty civilian aircraft searched in vain for the missing aircraft. Coast guard helicopters, Coast Guard Cutters, and spy aircraft were all used without success.

Both Congressmen were subsequently re-elected posthumously and Hale Boggs' wife, Lindy, would be appointed to serve out his term. Lindy would subsequently win re-election and remain in congress for the next eighteen years. The tragedy resulted in legislation mandating that all U.S. registered aircraft be equipped with emergency locator transmitters to aid search and rescue personnel in the event of a crash. Ironically, Congressman Boggs was driven to the airport to begin his trip by a young democrat named Bill Clinton. Years later, President Clinton would name Lindy Boggs as Ambassador to the Vatican when she retired from congress.

The implementation of the law would require years to develop the technology, manufacture, and test the new equipment. In 1978 the FAA was still in the process of requiring various segments of the industry to comply with the law, but fortunately, Rocky Mountain Airways had already installed the equipment and it was operational.

*****

One of the first actions by the Air Force Rescue Coordination Center was to notify the Colorado Wing of the Civil Air Patrol. In 1941, just one week before the December seventh bombing of Pearl Harbor, the CAP was formed and has continually served the nation with a dedicated volunteer force providing a variety of emergency services ever since. By an act of congress, the CAP is a civilian auxiliary of the United States Air Force and is assigned various missions, including search and rescue, by the Command Center.

The list of Colorado CAP personnel to be notified included Colorado Wing Emergency Services Officer, Earl Berger, Mission Coordinator, Sonny Elgin, and Ground Search and Rescue Team Leader, Jim Alsum.

Earl Berger immediately began establishing contact with all CAP search and rescue personnel in Denver via the FM radio alert system and by telephone. He was assisted by his wife Betty, also a CAP volunteer. It was 8:05 p.m. and the clock was ticking. The mission was on.

It was obvious that an airborne search was out of the question until sunrise and the weather cleared, but the darkness and weather would not deter the resolve of the ground search and rescue unit. Snow, wind, and ice were obstacles, but that's what the team trained for, and there was no hesitation. They prepared for a long cold night.

*****

Sgt. Jack Donner, of the Colorado State Patrol, was accustomed to patrolling the icy roads of Jackson and Grand Counties, and he had almost completed his twelve-hour day shift— hoping the radio would stay silent until he did. Blizzard conditions and frozen pavement usually combined to keep most residents at home which sometimes reduced his workload significantly—but not always. Sgt. Donner had left the State Patrol Station at Hot Sulphur Springs and was on his way home to Kremmling when his routine day—if there is such a thing in law enforcement—became much more complicated.

The dispatcher, back in Hot Sulphur Springs, radioed the alert that an airliner had possibly gone down east of Steamboat Springs, and that meant Sgt. Donner's duty day had just been extended indefinitely. His wife, Lonnie, would not be surprised or unduly alarmed when he didn't show up at the normal time. The evening news usually told her what event had delayed his arrival and a missing airliner would certainly explain his whereabouts.

Jack recalled the evening, "When I got the call, I turned around and headed north on Highway-Fourteen toward Walden where the search and rescue teams would be staging. Jackson County only had three full-time law enforcement officers at the time—Sheriff Ervin Swayze, the Walden City Marshall, and State Patrolman Jimmy Cure who normally covered the area.

"I came across several vehicles that had been abandoned along the highway due to the weather conditions and stopped to make sure no one was stranded inside. Snow was coming down hard and the windows were iced over. Snow drifts were over a foot deep and above the door jambs on the windward side of most cars, so I had to walk around to the lee side to check the interior of the vehicles. Fortunately, it seemed that everyone had found better transportation and just left the cars to be retrieved later.

"I continued on toward Walden to see how I could be of assistance to Sheriff Swayze. Jimmy Cure had founded and organized the Jackson County Search and Rescue team, and I knew he would be mapping out a plan."

*****

In Steamboat Springs, the emergency room at Routt Memorial Hospital was busy, as usual, with a variety of injuries and illnesses to be tended. The patients were in the capable hands of Doctor Larry Bookman, who was on duty and providing treatment and care for those in need. Larry had served as a Navy Flight Surgeon for three and a half years during the Vietnam War, including two tours in Southeast Asia. After his service to the country, he began a residency in Emergency Medicine at Denver General Hospital and worked at both level one trauma centers in the city.

In the winter of 1978, Doctor Bookman began traveling to Steamboat Springs on the weekends to fulfill the need for an Emergency Medicine Specialist at that hospital.

Larry remembered, "The night of the accident I got a call that an airplane was believed to have gone down near Buffalo Pass and was asked if I wanted to go on the search. I declined for two reasons. First, if I went, I would not have been available for anything that happened in town, and second, in my experience, an uncontrolled crash rarely had survivors. I told them that when the plane was found, and if there were survivors, I would go the scene."

It was still early in the evening and normally a busy time for the ER. Now that he was aware of the possibility that he might be needed, if the airplane was found, he continued to fulfill the immediate need in the emergency room while formulating a plan for the possibility of being called to the scene of the crash.

*****

When the remaining wreckage of the Twin Otter finally came to rest, the passenger cabin of the airliner had been instantly scrambled. Most of the seats had broken loose from the floor mounts, and the cabin was a jumble of seats and bodies. People and seats were piled on top of each other along with other debris, and a combination of shock and panic prevailed among the passengers. There had been no warning of the impending crash and it was totally unexpected. The crew had been completely occupied with trying to save the airplane, and they did not have the opportunity to use the public address system and there was no flight attendant to warn the passengers. By some miracle, or twist of fate, the ship's battery remained intact and continued to power the cabin lights. The illumination served to display a scene most would probably like to forget.

When Jon Pratt boarded the flight in Steamboat, he had taken the seat across from the passenger entrance door beside a young lady.

Jon said, "Immediately after we crashed, I was standing with the door now directly above me. I couldn't get the handle to work, so I took the safety card out of the seat pocket and tried to read it. I had a broken nose and a busted tooth, so I know I was suffering the effects of shock and could not consume the words or pictures. They were meaningless, and I could not understand anything on the card.

"One of the Forest Service ladies, who had been sitting behind me, was able to turn the handle but could not open the door because the heavy fold out stairs were part of it. Normally the assembly opened outward and down with the assistance of gravity, but now, since the airplane was on its side, we had to push the door and the stairs almost straight up into the sky."

Although it was difficult to open the door with the fuselage lying on its right side, it would have been disastrous if the cabin had rolled the opposite direction. With the passenger door and the baggage door on the left side, the passengers would have been trapped with no normal exits and no access to the baggage compartment.

Jon continued, "I'm sure adrenaline was involved, but I was able to push it open, jump out, and take off running. At least that was the plan until I realized I was in snow up to my crotch. I made about two steps and was done for. I was sure the airplane was going to explode like on TV. I was in flight mode and just wanted to get away. After trying a few more steps, I calmed my breathing and started to feel that maybe it wasn't going to blow up."

The aircraft's fuel tanks were located beneath the passenger seats in the belly of the fuselage; however, jet fuel is basically kerosene and not as flammable as gasoline and with the engines separated from the airplane there was no ignition source anyway. The airplane's oxygen tanks were probably a greater fire hazard but fortunately did not have an ignition source either.

Jon continued, "I had no idea that we had turned around and were going back to Steamboat. I started to look around because I thought we were right outside Golden or Denver, and I would surely see a road or house or something. I would just walk over and flag someone down.

"Then it hit me—we were in trouble."

Chapter 4

The Pine Grove Ranch restaurant in Steamboat Springs was a popular eatery and gathering place. Known for good food and friendly service, the establishment also featured a nice bar equipped with a TV so customers could watch the news or sports while enjoying a taste of something distilled before or after a nice meal.

Dave Lindow had been at the Pine Grove most of the evening, enjoying the warm atmosphere on a cold night—although he had yet to purchase anything to benefit the establishment. Some might have considered that he was loitering except for the fact that he owned the place. Dave was well established in Steamboat as an entrepreneur and business man. His primary endeavor was as a contractor and developer, but he was also a pilot and owned the local Fixed Based Operation at the airport. The FBO was a full-service facility and offered parking for airplanes, aircraft rental, flight instruction, as well as fuel. Dave owned several airplanes.

As part of his property development business, he found it necessary to access remote areas in the winter and thus had purchased a machine known as a snow cat to make that feasible. The snow cat was an enclosed cab, truck sized, fully tracked vehicle capable of traversing rough terrain in deep snow. Dave enjoyed the outdoors and like Jon Pratt, he had earned the status of Eagle Scout while growing up in Minnesota. He had taken the opportunity to explore the west side of Buffalo Pass in the snow cat and was familiar with the mountain. Dave was a community minded citizen, as most Eagle Scouts were, and volunteered for community service whenever called upon.

Dave's relaxed evening at the Pine Grove Ranch was interrupted when someone pointed to a local news anchor on TV who was reporting that Rocky Mountain Airways Flight 217 was overdue and presumed down. Air Traffic Control had lost contact with the airliner as it was inbound to Steamboat Springs.

Dave said, "I was at the restaurant that evening when I saw on the bar's TV, that the Rocky Flight was missing and possibly down in our area. At that point, I hustled down to our sheriff's office, as they were apparently in charge of the search and volunteered my help. Our local search and rescue organization was quite small and only had snowmobiles for equipment, which made them useless in a search of deep snow areas. I had the only privately owned snow cat in our area at the time and was quite familiar with the west side and top of the Buffalo Pass area from pioneering the powder slopes accessible only by snow cat."

When Dave arrived at the Sheriff's office, he learned they had been notified of the missing airplane at about 8:25 p.m. The sheriff had been informed about the ELT signal picked up by the Air Force C-130 near Walden. Search teams were being organized and dispatched to the Walden vicinity, located in the high plain of North Park. Unknown to anyone at the time, Gary Coleman also carried a personal ELT in his flight kit. The portable ELT had been a Christmas gift the previous year from his friend and fellow pilot, Ron Plunkett.

One or both of the instruments were now transmitting on the international emergency frequency. The sheriff quickly enlisted Dave and asked him to load the snow cat and head to Walden.

Dave said, "I had been flying in this area for years and expressed my opinion that it was unlikely the airplane would go down in the flat terrain around Walden. When someone mentioned that there had been a brief power outage due to a high voltage circuit breaker popping, I reminded the sheriff that the power lines ran over Buffalo Pass, and it was possible the power surge had been caused by the airplane crash. He asked that I go to Walden and wait for further word so I prepared to do what he wanted.

"He suggested I team up with Ed Duncan who had also volunteered. Ed worked for Greeley Gas Company and just happened to have a flatbed trailer already rigged and ready to go. That would save us time since I wouldn't have to hook up my trailer to haul the snow cat. Ed and I gathered the gear and equipment we needed, loaded the snow cat, and headed out."

*****

When Maureen Redmond boarded the flight in Steamboat, she had taken the aisle seat next to Margie Kotts and her eight-month old son, Matthew. Maureen said, "I was nervous before and during the flight. I proceeded to get into the crash position for takeoff and stayed there for most of the flight. I occasionally peeked past Margie to see out the window. Zero visibility—only swirling snow. The flight was very smooth but seemed long to me. We were not told that we were attempting to return to Steamboat Springs.

"After about fifty minutes or so, the flight started getting bumpy and I was relieved because I thought we were beginning our descent into Denver and were being tossed around a bit by the different layers of air.

"There was suddenly an incredibly bright flash of light and almost simultaneously a sensation of being thrown down and crushed by a giant hand. I blacked out for a brief time and when I became conscious, I was fighting to get to the exit. My mind was thinking fire. It was like my body was moving before my mind commanded it to. I'm still not sure how that happened. I realized I was stepping all over other people, and someone was grabbing me and saying it was going to be okay. I think it was Jon Pratt who tried to calm me down.

"The inside of the plane was just a jumbled pile of seats and bodies. I think all the seats came loose. Maybe they are supposed to so the seat belt doesn't cut you in half. There was no way to make sense of it.

"Some woman in the back said, 'Hey, I found this kid. Where did this kid come from?' It was Matthew. I told her to pass him up to me because I was near his mom."

Margie had dressed Matt in a nice thick snow suit to keep him warm during the trip and when he was tossed around during the crash, the snow suit cushioned and protected him.

Maureen continued, "When I looked at Margie, she was unconscious. I had seven siblings, and I knew I was the best person to take care of Matt. I checked to make sure he was conscious and that his eyes were focusing. I jiggled him around to keep him awake in case he had a concussion."

*****

The Denver unit of the Civil Air Patrol mobilized quickly. Earl and Betty Berger were hard at work coordinating the mission.

Both were experienced and well qualified for the task. Earl was an electronic engineer by profession and a natural fit for maintaining and operating the radio equipment necessary to direct the search teams. He had served the United States Navy as a bombardier during World War II and was now also qualified as a mission pilot and aircraft mechanic with CAP. In addition to the radio equipment, Earl and Betty had installed two telephones in their home. One for incoming calls during a mission, and another for outgoing calls.

Betty was also a pilot and lifelong aviation enthusiast. She grew up in the 1930's and remembered taking her first airplane ride with a barnstorming pilot who visited her small town in South Dakota.

"The experience was scary, fascinating, and enlightening for a preschooler. My interest in aviation was renewed with Amelia Earhart's last flight and disappearance in 1937. Amelia was the first president of The Ninety-Nines Inc. an organization formed in 1929 to encourage mutual support and achievement for female pilots. It was so named because 99 of the 117 licensed female pilots in the United States attended the first meeting.

"When I learned to fly in the late 1960's, I joined the Ninety-Nines. One of the club's activities was the annual all female cross country air race called the Powder Puff Derby. With my husband Earl's encouragement, my friend, Jennifer Caine and I participated in a race from Redding, Ca. to Orlando, Fla. That was definitely an educational experience."

Intense training was required to participate in Civil Air Patrol missions and Earl and Betty had plenty of experience. In the 1970's, CAP was averaging about 50 search missions a year in Colorado alone.

Betty recalled, "On the evening of December the fourth, 1978, Earl received a call from the Air Force Rescue Coordination Center that a commercial aircraft was missing between Steamboat Springs and Denver with twenty-two people on board. Weather conditions in the mountains included high winds, snow, and extremely cold temperature. We immediately started making the required notifications and coordinating with Jim Alsum with the CAP Ground Search and Rescue Team, and Sonny Elgin, Mission Coordinator."

Leaving no stone unturned, Earl and Betty were even calling people who lived along the route of flight to see if they had seen or heard anything unusual.

Betty said, "Communications were difficult—FM (frequency modulated) radios had a limited range, and HF (high frequency) radios could be noisy and unreliable. There were no cell phones at the time."

*****

Vern Bell remembers the flight, "The takeoff from Steamboat seemed normal and I thought the flight was routine, but after a while in the air, there was a good amount of turbulence. I could tell the plane was having a problem with icing as pieces of ice would break loose from the propellers and slam into the side of the plane. I could tell the plane was having some trouble with the altitude since the pilot seemed to be battling downdrafts and trying to keep the nose up. I had experienced problems with strong winds one time before. My father was a pilot and was flying us in a Beech Bonanza aircraft and we were landing in Las Vegas. It seemed to be very similar—strong side gusts and downdrafts.

"We didn't know we were going to crash, and the last thing I remember, just a split second before impact, was a flash of light. That may have been from the aircraft's landing lights against the snow, or us hitting a power line, or perhaps it was just the blow to my head from hitting the seat in front of me.

"The next thing I remember was Jon Pratt hovering over me and telling me we had crashed. I was knocked out, but I don't remember for how long. I was very dazed for a while, but I was able to get to my feet and gather some of my senses. I had a gash on my right brow where my head hit the seat in front of me, and my thumb was gashed open also. It was so surreal for a time…like being in a dream…not really knowing if it was real or not. I was woozy but made my way out of the airplane and found myself waist deep in snow."

*****

37

The ground search team was on the move. Jim Alsum had been assigned as mission team leader, and he notified his crew and went into action. Not only did the volunteer team train together for CAP missions, most of them worked for Jim Alsum in his construction business. As such, they were outdoorsmen and physically and mentally tough. They did not shrink from a challenge. In fact, as with most good friends and team members, they drove each other in friendly competition. Each of them knew their team mates were predictable and dependable. The team included Jim's two sons, Jerry, and Dan, and also Don Niekerk and Rick Hopp. The close knit friends worked hard all week and attended church together on Sunday. They had faith in each other and faith that God would lead them in their life. On this frigid Colorado night, they would be joined by fellow CAP members Sonny Elgin and Harry Blakeman.

Jim Alsum had been conducting search and rescue for CAP since 1968—ten years prior to the crash of Flight 217. He had been motivated to get involved by a family tragedy involving a private airplane crash.

Jim said, "In 1963 we lost a cousin, a brother-in-law and his brother, and one of their company employees. They flew from Denver to Alamosa in a Cessna 182 on a business trip. On the return trip, they were flying with lowering cloud conditions with no instrument flying experience and they were low time pilots. When they became overdue that night, we only had questions, but no one to give us answers. Were they down in open land, or in the mountains, or in a lake? Were they alive, or suffering, or no longer with us? What should we do, or who should we call?

"The next morning, I called a friend who owned a Cessna 210 and asked for his help. We learned that Civil Air Patrol had set up a search base at Pueblo, and we landed there to give them as much information as we could. We then searched until we ran low on fuel and had to return to Denver. We called the tower and asked if they knew anything about the missing aircraft, and they gave us a phone number to call. We learned that the airplane had been found, and they gave us the location. When we reached the crash scene, it was horrifying and I'll never forget it—seeing your family members in conditions you never expected to see them in. I'll never forget that feeling or that vision.

"The accident left ten children without fathers. That experience, and seeing what a family goes through, stayed with me for years, and in 1968, I joined Civil Air Patrol Emergency Services Division and focused on starting a ground search team to work with the air search teams."

Over the next 32 years, Jim's team would work over 300 missing aircraft missions and over 500 ELT searches. They assisted many sheriff departments in searching for lost persons as well. Jim also became a mission pilot and later became the Director of Emergency Services for the Colorado Wing of Civil Air Patrol.

Jim remembers the Flight 217 crash and indicates, "The summer before the 217 accident, our team had built a search and rescue trailer. Someone donated a chassis to us, and the guys would come over in the evening after work to construct it. We made it seven feet wide, eight feet long, and four feet tall. The purpose was to carry any team equipment that we thought we would need on a search or rescue mission.

"The trailer contained a wire rescue basket or Stokes litter along with a high flotation wheel and tire to put under the basket to allow it to be wheeled down a trail. It also contained a fiberglass snow boat similar to those used by Ski Patrol teams to move an injured skier down the mountain. It had four wooden backboards, a three burner propane stove, a five-gallon jug of fresh water, three one gallon pots for heating water, climbing equipment including a couple of 300-foot climbing/rescue ropes, three down casualty bags, a dozen army blankets, and an oxygen kit. We would need everything we had the night of the Rocky Mountain Airways crash.

"We received the mission alert a little after eight p.m. and began organizing the team and equipment. We knew the emergency locator transmitter had been detected east of Steamboat Springs and our first objective was to get to the city of Kremmling and then try to track it down. The road conditions were bad and the weather conditions in the mountains would be even worse."

*****

Dan Alsum said, "When my brother Jerry and I were young, dad gave us many opportunities to experience outdoor activities. We played sports in school and naturally loved being outdoors. We enjoyed backpacking, camping, four-wheeling, and rock climbing. We developed an early bond of doing things together. Not only did we play together, we worked together in the construction business my father owned. I had just graduated from high school in May of 1978 and was happy to be starting my career as a fourth generation builder and learning from my dad and older brother.

"Dad had been involved in search and rescue for many years prior to December, 1978. Our extended family had experienced the tragedy of an airplane crash that left wives and children without husbands and fathers. After that, dad felt a calling to help other families in their time of need during a crisis. Search and rescue became his passion. Jerry and I became involved in our late teenage years and put our outdoor skills to good use as we learned the organizational skills required for team development. Friends joined our team not only at work but also at Civil Air Patrol.

"On December 4, 1978, Jerry, Rick Hopp, and I were trimming out the interior of a custom home that was near completion. After work, I was spending the evening at home with mom and dad watching Monday Night Football. The San Diego Chargers were playing the Chicago Bears. It was cold and snowing in Denver. When the phone rang, I answered and it was the Air Force Rescue Coordination Center (AFRCC) calling for Jim Alsum. I put dad on the phone and we found out Rocky Mountain Airways Flight 217, bound from Steamboat to Denver, was presumed down with twenty-two souls on board. Mom immediately began preparing coffee and food. She never let us leave home without making sure we had what we needed."

*****

Jerry Alsum said, "I was at home after working all day on a house my dad was building. My wife was five months pregnant with our first child, and she had been attending nursing school. She had been doing her clinical rotations at various hospitals in the Denver area, one of which was Saint Anthony. It was about eight o'clock at night, and I had settled in to watch Monday Night Football, when my dad called and said an airliner type airplane had gone down in the mountains. He said to come to his house and prepare to head out on the search. My wife was less than pleased about me leaving, but I explained that this was a big plane and lots of lives could be at risk. I left in a rush.

"I hurriedly packed all my personal gear in my vehicle and started the ten-mile drive to my dad's house. The team's search and rescue trailer was located in dad's garage, along with our other SAR gear. My brother, Dan, was already there, and the three of us began loading the trailer and Dan's Blazer."

*****

Don Niekerk remembered, "I got a call from Dan Alsum that night, and he told me about the missing airliner. He asked me to meet them at his house as soon as possible. I put my gear together and hurried to meet with Jim, Dan, and Jerry, and we began loading up. We hitched a trailer to Dan's four-wheel drive and loaded two snowmobiles and a tow behind sled. We hitched the rescue trailer with all our equipment to Jim's four-wheel drive. I threw my gear into Jim's SUV to ride with him, and Jerry and Dan loaded their gear in Dan's Blazer. Jim told us that an ELT signal had been picked up by aircraft flying overhead east of Steamboat Springs, and we were heading to Kremmling to meet other CAP personnel. I attached two magnetic mounted antennas to the roof of Jim's SUV, which allowed us to use the ELT direction finding equipment while driving."

At the same time, Rick Hopp was loading his snowmobile and other gear in his truck at his home. The plan was to meet Rick, Sonny Elgin, and Harry Blakeman in Idaho Springs as they made their way toward Kremmling.

The small Civil Air Patrol convoy headed west on Interstate Seventy through a steady snowfall. They knew the snow would become heavier when they reached the front range and started the climb. Traffic was light and they made steady progress as the CAP radios chattered with planning and coordination. Earl and Betty Berger were passing along information as they received it. Jerry Alsum, Don Niekerk, Rick Hopp, and Dan Alsum felt their internal clock ticking. They had all trained as EMTs (emergency medical technician) and knew that every minute was critical.

*****

Sonny Elgin remembers, "I was at home, just starting to watch MASH on TV, when a call came in from the Air Force Rescue Coordination Center (AFRCC) at Scott AFB in Illinois. The controllers at Scott were still talking to controllers at Denver Center who were still trying to contact Flight 217. While on the phone, I put out a radio message on the Civil Air Patrol net, notifying members in the Denver area of a possible Rocky Mountain flight down somewhere east of Steamboat Springs. Jim Alsum, Harry Blakeman, Earl Berger, and several others immediately responded. After a short time, AFRCC issued an Air Force mission number and CAP members began to mobilize.

"This mission was very special and important to me, as I was born and raised in Steamboat Springs. My father taught me to fly at the Steamboat airport, where he had built the original airstrip. Having grown up in Steamboat, I was very familiar with the local area. This familiarity would prove very helpful in the search for this downed aircraft.

"I left my home near Watkins, Colorado and proceeded to a rendezvous point with other searchers at the Safeway parking lot in Idaho Springs. As I drove across the Denver area, I was in radio contact with Harry Blakeman, who was covering a large fire at Rocky Flats for his employer, Channel Nine News in Denver. I think Harry was the first to arrive at the Safeway. When everyone had gathered at the staging point in Idaho Springs, we all proceeded westbound on I-70 through the Eisenhower tunnel to Silverthorne, then north on Colorado Highway Nine to Kremmling. It was snowing hard and blowing hard the whole way."

*****

Harry Blakeman was a man of diverse background and experience. He became a licensed radio operator at age fifteen and began training as an auxiliary firefighter the same year. Rules being what they were, he was not allowed to fight fires until he turned sixteen, and then only if he did not enter a burning building.

At seventeen he joined the U.S. Airforce and became an electronics technician. His interest in electronics and aircraft continued, and he was assigned to research and development for new aircraft systems. As such he was required to maintain a minimum monthly number of flight hours as a crewmember and was trained in egress from fighter jets as well as search and rescue procedures in C-130 aircraft. In his spare time, he served as the training officer for a volunteer fire department near his base in Florida.

Harry explains, "Later, in 1969, I was reassigned to Lowry Air Force Base in Denver where I was an instructor in electronic systems. I joined the Alpine Rescue Team in Evergreen and provided radio communications for them during their search and rescue incidents using amateur radio equipment. At that time, volunteer rescue teams did not have their own radios due to the cost involved."

Harry recalls one of his earlier and more memorable missions and states, "On October 2, 1970, I was alerted to respond to a report of a large aircraft crashing on the north side of Interstate Seventy about eight miles west of Silver Plume. Ironically, an amateur radio operator in Georgetown radioed me that he saw a large aircraft flying up the canyon at a low altitude, and he did not think the airplane would be able to make it over the Continental Divide. That aircraft was a Martin 404 leased by Wichita State University from Golden Eagle Aviation to fly their football team to a game in Utah. The pilot had decided to take the *scenic route* and was using a Denver sectional chart so he could point out landmarks to the players and coaches.

"There were forty people on board and twenty-nine perished on scene in the crash and resulting fire. Many were injured during the impact but were unable to get out before it caught fire. Two others died at the hospital. The aircraft had just refueled at Stapleton Airport in Denver and had a large quantity of fuel on board. Radio communications from the crash site in the canyon were difficult but workable. We learned a lot about crisis radio in the next two days. The phone company was eventually able to string a phone cable up the side of the mountain to near the rear of the wreckage to provide a single telephone for the Colorado State Patrol to use.

"In 1971 I left the Air Force and went to work as a radio news reporter and TV photojournalist at KBTR radio and KBTV in Denver. As a news person, I covered many incidents involving aircraft and search and rescue. ELTs were coming into existence and I continued to learn more about radio direction finding. I converted a surplus military aircraft radio for use in my home and my vehicle so I could locate ELTs that were activated. I participated in amateur radio direction finding competitions in the Denver area and became proficient enough to come in first about half the time. That's where I met Lt. Col. Harry Kouts who was Director of Communications for the Colorado Wing of the Civil Air Patrol. He asked me if I would consider joining the CAP as they were in need of a Public Information Officer.

"After joining CAP, I branched out into communications and emergency services and worked a lot of missing aircraft searches with Lt. Col. Sonny Elgin. I learned a lot and could not have asked for a better mentor than Sonny. I became a mission coordinator and eventually the Colorado Wing Emergency Services Officer, the position Sonny held prior to me. Along the way I met Jim Alsum who was a member of the Littleton Senior Squadron. Jim and his son Jerry were very active in ground search and as I recall, Dan was just seventeen and not old enough to be a senior member yet. I asked Jim if he would join my staff and perform ground team training for the entire state. Jim agreed and the premier ground team was grown and their training and real mission accomplishments grew along with them."

On December the fourth, 1978, Harry thought his day was almost done when he finished his day shift as a radio electronics technician at the City of Aurora. Little did he know it was just beginning. "After work, I drove to downtown Denver to pick up some electronics parts. It was windy downtown but nothing extreme at the time. In 1978, weather forecasts and the dissemination of that information was nowhere near the level it would become in later years. One thing I learned after moving to Colorado in 1964 was that the downslope winds coming off the foothills west of Denver in December and January easily reached seventy to ninety miles an hour and occasionally more.

"I was freelancing as a photojournalist with Channel Nine News, and as I returned to my vehicle with the parts, I heard a fire dispatched by the Arvada Fire Department for a wind driven fire in a commercial building in the area south of the Rocky Flats plutonium processing facility. When I arrived at the fire to film for Nine News, I could barely get the door of my vehicle open. The wind must have been seventy to eighty miles an hour. After documenting the fire on film, which must have taken about two hours, I returned to my vehicle about eight o'clock just as Sonny Elgin's voice came over the Civil Air Patrol radio. Sonny said something like, 'All Civil Air Patrol stations standby for a mission involving an overdue commercial aircraft west of Denver.' Already being on the far west side of metro Denver, I knew I would be one of the first CAP members to head west once we had a better location.

"There would not be time to return to my residence to pick up supplies before heading to the crash site, but I always kept extra winter clothing and military MRE type food in my vehicle. My SUV was outfitted as a mobile communications platform with sixteen radios and thirteen external antennas mounted to the body. In addition to the CAP radios, I had amateur radios and a two-way radio on the national search and rescue channel and on the Colorado State Patrol statewide emergency channel. I could also listen to the communications of the various sheriff's offices, State Patrol, snowplows, and other search and rescue teams in the area. Additionally, I had a Citizen's Band radio to get road reports from truckers and to talk to anyone who might have seen a flash in the sky or some other visual or sound making clue.

"Sonny Elgin had received the alert notification from the Air Force Rescue Coordination Center and was on the phone getting the few details that were initially available. Very soon we knew it was Flight 217 and that it had likely gone down between North Park, south of Walden, and Steamboat Springs.

"CAP members including Jim Alsum and his ground team, Earl and Betty Berger, Sonny Elgin, and myself were in nearly constant contact on the CAP FM radio making plans for the response as the information on Flight 217 continued to come in. We needed to make sure all of our response coordination, particularly with the Bergers, was complete before we drove out of radio range. Other than myself, only Jim Alsum had a high frequency (HF) radio in his vehicle that would allow communication with stations in the Denver area from a greater distance. The HF antennas on our vehicles were only seven-feet long and sometimes resulted in a weak signal.

Harrison Jones

"I went to the fire station in Idaho Springs to pick up supplies and hoped to hook up with Gene Day, another CAP member. Gene was a law enforcement officer, a volunteer firefighter, and a radio operator, but unfortunately, he had to work and couldn't go with us. As Sonny and Jim and his team approached Idaho Springs, we were in radio contact and decided to meet at the Safeway store on I-70 to pick up more supplies. Unfortunately, the Safeway was closed by the time we got there."

Chapter 5

Rocky Mountain Airway's headquarters and general offices were located at Stapleton International Airport in Denver. On the evening of December fourth, 1978, Dennis Heap was on duty and managing his responsibilities.

"I was Rocky Mountain Airway's Vice President of Passenger Services with my office in Hangar Six at Stapleton; however, I lived in Steamboat Springs as I had started that station. As was my custom, I flew down from Steamboat that morning and would return to Steamboat on the turnaround flight of 217.

"I knew flight 217 was running late, which meant my flight to Steamboat would be late, so I waited until around seven p.m. to drive from Hangar Six to the terminal parking lot, then on to Gate A-3 to check in for Flight 218. Normally the forty-five-minute flight got me home in time to have dinner, watch a little TV, and get to bed at a reasonable time, but that was when the flight left on time at six p.m.

"I made a practice of arriving at Concourse 'A' early so I could visit with dispatch, and the gate and ramp agents. It was an RMA practice to 'manage by walking around.' It was Monday, which meant the loads wouldn't be as heavy as on a weekend, but a quick walkthrough of the bag room, ramp and gates conveyed how well the overall operation was going. Dispatch was the heart of the operation as they knew where each aircraft was, as well as current and forecast weather. That's when I learned that 217 had diverted back to Steamboat.

"In addition to stations operations, I was responsible for reservations and flight scheduling. Therefore, I was responsible for rescheduling, rerouting, etc. I returned to Hangar Six, where our reservations office was located and began working with various managers on a new game plan. With only seven aircraft in our fleet, scheduling was very tight. We had one of the industry's highest daily aircraft utilization rates with each of our aircraft averaging 11.5 flight hours a day. All seven aircraft were scheduled to return to Denver every night so maintenance could be performed on the entire fleet under one roof at Hangar Six. Denver was a connecting hub for most of our passengers, and all aircraft would be back in the air by seven the next morning.

"When it became apparent that the situation was more serious than a diversion back to Steamboat, and we had possibly lost our aircraft, I put on my damage control hat as I was responsible for communications with the press, and I was also the central coordinator for incidents and accidents. The president of the airline, Gordon Autry, Vice President of Flight Operations, Bruce Gunberg, and myself all received constant updates from dispatch on the status of Flight 217 including news of its last radio transmission.

"We began rerouting, cancelling, and delaying flights to compensate for losing one of our six Twin Otters. Reservation agents called passengers and rebooked flights. Flight Operations redid their schedule for crews and called in reserve pilots. Stations made adjustments to their staffing schedules and while all of that was going on, everyone shared a common anxiety for the outcome of Flight 217 and the passengers and crew.

"I worked with Patty Bell, our Manager of Reservations and a small but efficient staff through the night on the second floor of Hangar Six. From time to time we would look out the row of interior windows to the hangar floor below, where RMA mechanics were using tugs to back our one Dash-7 and five Twin Otters into place for the night's maintenance routine. Missing a night of sleep is easy when you are propelled by adrenaline and the employees are young. I was thirty-four years old at the time and somewhat senior in age to those I worked with. The night was spent in emergency mode and like a pilot who is experiencing an emergency, training and natural instincts guided everyone's actions and thoughts. We were busy with scheduling for the next day, receiving and passing on updates, and talking with relatives of the passengers on Flight 217, which kept us from thinking about the worse-case scenario."

*****

The news media were not only calling Dennis Heap. They had gathered enough information to go live and competed with each other to offer the latest information. The missing flight was the lead story on the ten o'clock news, and the scramble was on to find local

48

aviation experts to offer opinions. Most credible sources declined to speculate.

The breaking news story was broadcast into living rooms all over Colorado and surrounding states by the local affiliates and was soon picked up by the national networks and wire services. An airplane crash seems to grab everyone's attention like no other news story.

Maybe it's because it happens so rarely.

Maybe it's because it leaves everyone wondering who was on the flight.

Maybe it's because the varying speculation, as to the cause, creates a mystery that must be solved.

Maybe it's because some can't resist the mental image of burning wreckage and mangled bodies, and wait anxiously for photos, live video, and eyewitness accounts.

Maybe it's because humans are…well…humans.

*****

In Denver, Jim Alsum's wife, Lorraine, watched the news and waited for information about the CAP team. Jerry Alsum's wife, Janice, watched and wondered if her husband was safe.

In Boulder, Colorado, the news brought shock and distress to the home of Harvey and Marcella Coleman. The couple had three sons, Bill, Don, and Gary. All three were pilots. Gary had dropped by to visit his parents on his way to the airport earlier in the day, and he had mentioned that he would be flying to Steamboat later in the afternoon. The two parents were stunned by the news report but recovered enough to call Don in Estes Park, and Bill in Park City, Utah.

Don Coleman recalls, "I visited my parents on that Monday morning before Gary's flight. The winds in the foothills were hurricane strength. Driving through Clear Creek Canyon on my way to their home in Boulder, I almost got nailed by huge rocks blowing off the mountain. I was visiting with mom and dad when Gary stopped by on his way to Stapleton for his flight. I didn't know he was flying that day or stopping by. Mom was so concerned about the weather, but Gary said he had his wool socks and wool pants on and not to worry. He told dad that he had his emergency locator transmitter in his flight bag.

"I asked him where he was flying and he said Steamboat. As he went out the door, we looked at each other for a long moment in silence. I quietly said they would probably cancel all mountain flights today."

*****

The Coleman brothers grew up on a farm in Iowa and had been fascinated by airplanes since an early age. In the summer they would climb on top of the chicken coop or the silo and watch crop dusters swoop down from the sky to skim the fields and release their chemicals. Their mother expected as much from Bill and Gary but was not happy that they encouraged their baby brother, Don, to follow them.

Bill Coleman remembered, "It was around nine p.m. when I received the phone call. When both Mom and Dad were on the phone, I knew it was serious. That usually meant an emergency, or a relative passing, or a dear friend...but not about Gary. They told me all they knew, which wasn't much, but the darkness of the situation was clear. The plane was overdue and feared down. Those were the facts. But in the middle of the night, in a winter ice storm, near Rabbit Ears Pass, with no civilization nearby? The news only left my imagination to mess with me.

"Growing up on the farm in Iowa, Gary and I were always invincible. Our childhood heroic play, our same heroes, our swashbuckling daring—always snatching victory from defeat. But now it was Gary in trouble.

"I was several hundred miles away and felt helpless, but I could think of nothing but Gary. When I was about eight years old, Mom and Dad took us to the drive-in to see John Wayne in the classic aviation movie, *The High and the Mighty*. I had to learn to whistle like the heroic character. I remembered another John Wayne classic called *Island in the Sky* where the hero overcame adversity, including the wings icing up, to save the airplane.

"I imagined Gary struggling to save the airplane, the passengers, and himself like John Wayne did in the movie. I refused

50

to consider any other outcome. I naturally chose the heroic conclusion like we did as kids on the farm. There had to be a John Wayne landing in there somewhere. I was the first to learn to fly and my two brothers followed soon thereafter. Gary took it all the way to the professional level, and he was a great pilot. I told myself that he would never give up—and I believed it."

*****

Ron Plunkett was at home when he saw the breaking news story announcing the missing Rocky Mountain Airways flight from Steamboat. Ron was a pilot and flight instructor, and also Gary Coleman's best friend.

Ron said, "I met Gary, and his brother Don, in the summer of 1969 when they bought a Cessna 150 and needed a flight instructor to teach them to fly. I gave them flying lessons and have felt like a brother since. The Coleman's were a very giving and caring family—always looking out for someone else rather than themselves.

"I was listening to the ten p.m. evening news, and they announced that a Rocky Mountain flight from Steamboat was late and suspected down. I knew Gary was flying to Steamboat that Monday. I hurried to his parent's home and knocked on the door. I could hear his mom and dad inside, but no one would come to the door—so I just went in. Harvey later told me that they thought I was the bearer of bad news, and they just couldn't respond. He told me Don was on his way to Boulder from Estes Park.

"Don arrived shortly and we decided we'd try to get to the area where they thought the plane might be. The power hiccup had already been reported, so the plane was suspected to be somewhere between Walden and Steamboat. We only hesitated long enough to convince Gary's dad not to go with us.

"I went home and got winter gear, snowshoes, and cross country skis and hurried back to the Coleman's and piled it all into Don's four-wheel drive Land Cruiser. I made a call to my CAP contacts for the latest search update—then Don and I headed west. It was after eleven p.m. and the entire area was experiencing a bad storm, so our travel was slow. It was blizzard conditions and even though Don and I had traveled those roads many times, it was hard to sometimes tell where we were. We slid off the road more than a handful of times, and with the heater running full blast, we were still in Parkas."

*****

In 1943 a gentleman by the name of Abraham Maslow produced a study in psychology titled *Maslow's Hierarchy of Human Needs*. Maslow theorized that humans must meet a level of basic personal needs before they are able to advance to more satisfying needs and fulfill their potential in life. He divided human needs into five levels with the first having to be met before an individual could consider moving to the next. He illustrated his theory in the form of a pyramid. The first level to be achieved included air, food, water, sleep, shelter, and warmth. Once those needs were met, an individual could move on to safety, security, law, order, sense of belonging, etc. Ultimately the goal would be to reach the top of the pyramid and self-actualization—one's full potential in life.

Had Maslow been a passenger on Rocky Mountain Airways Flight 217, he could have experienced his theory in action and written several more books. It is doubtful if any of the twenty-two souls on board had ever struggled for air, food, water, shelter, or warmth. At least those basic needs had never been in jeopardy for long. Even at eight months old, Matt Kotts' needs had been provided by his parents, and with his mother, Margie, incapacitated, Maureen Redmond had assumed that responsibility, even though she had little to offer other than compassion and body heat. Until now, these people were accomplished and successful, well on their way to self-actualization. Each of them had elevated himself or herself in Maslow's hierarchy— he or she had experienced life, accomplished goals successfully, and he or she had the satisfaction of knowing they were loved and important to family and friends.

In a matter of seconds, their aircraft had fallen to the ground, and they had descended to the bottom of Maslow's pyramid of human needs. The air was breathable but frigid and dangerous to exposed skin. Little or no food or water. Minimal shelter but absolutely no warmth or comfort. No safety or security. No order—only confusion and chaos initially and then fear and suffering. Nowhere to run to. No privacy—not even a restroom for physiological needs.

They had no way of knowing that twenty minutes after the crash Jim Alsum had his search and rescue team moving. They could not know that Jim's team, as well as Sonny Elgin and Harry Blakeman, would not rest or sleep until their mission was complete. They were not aware that Dave Lindow and Ed Duncan were hauling a snow cat out of Steamboat and over Rabbit Ears Pass, despite the treacherous weather. They had no idea that Dr. Larry Bookman was on standby with a plan for their medical needs. They were unaware of, and could not hear, the little emergency locator transmitter radioing the relentless wail of the distress signal to anyone listening on the emergency frequency.

They wouldn't starve or thirst to death right away, and in fact, they might freeze to death before that happened. Some of the injuries were severe, and many of the survivors were unconscious or incoherent and unable to help themselves. They needed hope that only knowledge and leadership could bring. They needed someone or something to believe in—someone to instill the confidence that they would survive.

*****

Jon Pratt stood in waist deep snow and braced himself against the wind. He finally concluded the airplane was not going to explode.

"A quick survey of the situation indicated there were no lights revealing signs of civilization anywhere in sight. The power line we had hit with the right wingtip was buzzing and hissing as the snow continued to fall on the line. I invested a few seconds of brainpower on how we might break the power line. I figured if that line was broken, someone would come pretty quickly to fix it and find us. On the other hand, it was a good fifty feet in the air, likely had 200,000 volts of electricity passing through it, and was at the end of a long support arm. I put that thought aside for tomorrow when daylight came. Right now it was about getting through the night.

"Growing up in the mountains of Colorado, I knew of many stories, from the news, about small airplanes that were lost in the mountains and not found until years later. I knew we were in for a long haul. Survival was not a matter of hours—it was going to be days. I didn't want to think beyond a few days. It was snowing like crazy, it was cold, it was very windy, and of course, we were in deep snow.

"There was a small light on the outside of the door I had just jumped out of, and I could see that the main part of the airplane was essentially intact. The nose section forward of the cockpit and the wings were gone, but the tail was still attached. A wing was under the airplane and sticking out about a foot above the snow. The nose was uphill and above the snow, while the tail was downhill and mostly buried in the snow. Then there was the fact the passenger cabin was on its right side. My brain was in overdrive processing what had happened and what to do next. I had no clue what the status of the other passengers might be, but I knew if I or anyone else were to survive the night, and before I could offer my assistance to others, I would need some warmer clothes.

"Then I remembered the bag I had packed with a down parka, ski gloves, and a wool hat. I had watched it being loaded in the rear baggage compartment in Steamboat. Staying warm was my first priority, and I waded through the snow to open the baggage compartment door. A light automatically came on inside the compartment when I opened the door, and I crawled inside to start looking for my bag.

"Another passenger came up to the door and I could tell he had been stunned and was probably suffering from shock. 'Hi, I'm Vern Bell, I'm from Lakewood. I'm Vern Bell, I'm from Lakewood. I'm Vern Bell, I'm from Lakewood.'

"After the third time I interrupted him and said, "Listen Vern, I'm Jon Pratt, I'm from Steamboat. We've got to help these people because they're injured and we're all right. Can you help me toss these clothes into the plane? Just tell people to put on any clothes they can and cover up.

"Vern's face was covered in blood, but it did not appear to be flowing. He seemed to be more coherent now and gave a bit of a nod that he understood. Starting with the bag in my hand, I just opened each suitcase, took out anything that looked like clothing, handed them to Vern, and we had an assembly line underway with Vern handing the clothes to Cathy Williams, one of the Forest Service ladies, just inside the passenger cabin door. One of the bags had a bathrobe in it and I thought *who packs a bathrobe?* But on the other hand, I had packed a down sleeping bag. I kept the belt from the robe and then handed it to Vern. The empty suitcases were discarded on the snow outside the baggage compartment door.

"I finally found my bag, put on my hat, gloves, and the down parka, then removed the down sleeping bag I had packed and handed it to Vern. I told him to put someone in this who is really hurt. At that point I really had no idea of the status of the rest of the passengers or crew. All I knew was that I could hear a lot of moans and cries for help coming from the cabin."

*****

Maureen Redmond described the scene right after the crash. "Thank goodness the cabin lights stayed on. After I made sure the baby was okay, I realized there were injured people all around me. The worst ones were head injuries and people who were unconscious and thrashing all over. I know they couldn't help the state they were in, but they were injuring other people. I was not injured at all except my head bump. I think the fact that I was in the crash position saved me from getting hurt any worse.

"One lady had a bone sticking out of her lower leg and I said, 'Wow you have a bone sticking out of your leg!' I realized later that I must have been in shock to say something like that. She probably realized she had a bone sticking out of her leg and was scared and horrified by it. I don't remember calling to my friends, but I knew Cathy seemed okay and Mary Kay was unconscious and not responding.

"Someone got into the baggage compartment and began emptying luggage to give everyone what they could to stay warm. Matthew and I wound up with someone's robe and I settled in, snuggled up with him. There was a huge hole right where I was sitting where the wing ripped off. Margie was basically lying in the snow and unconscious, but I kept checking to make sure she was breathing okay. I tried to wrap her up as best I could and found what I thought was a large piece of white plastic to cover the hole and keep the snow out. As I was stuffing it into the opening, I realized it was the wedding dress of the really sweet couple who were flying to get married."

*****

Jeff Mercer and his fiancé, Luann, were seated together on the right side of the cabin forward of the wing. With no warning of the impending crash, they both sustained head injuries at impact. With the airplane now on its side, they were lying together against the wall of the cabin. Luann found herself trapped with her feet and legs pinned under a seat. Although his breathing seemed to be okay, Jeff was unconscious and would remain so throughout the night due to the head trauma and concussion he had suffered. He thrashed about uncontrollably and his feet kicked against Luann who was in severe pain and horrified to see a broken bone protruding from her right leg. Every instinct told her to run—get out of the airplane. However, she could not move, and she could not help Jeff.

All around her people were injured and calling for help. In the dim glow of the cabin lights, all she could see was devastation and destruction. Somehow a cold wind had found its way into the cabin, and unexplainably she could hear a baby cry.

Then she discovered that her left leg was bleeding from a severe gash. She wondered if her and Jeff's families would ever know what happened to them.

Chapter 6

Patty Bell was nearing the end of her day shift at Stapleton Airport in Denver and looking forward to a pleasant evening at home with her husband. Patty was a former elementary school teacher who enjoyed a challenge, and when she had the opportunity to become involved in the travel industry, she never looked back. Her title was Manager of Reservations Sales and Service for Rocky Mountain Airways, and the weather had played havoc with the airline's schedules all day. Flight delays and cancelations created a dreaded situation in the airline business known as *irregular operations*. For Patty, and the personnel she supervised, that meant hours and hours of *re-accommodating* inconvenienced passengers. Rocky Mountain Airways did not have an abundance of spare airplanes sitting around, and when one flight canceled, it affected all the flights that airplane was scheduled to fly the rest of the day. The problem was compounded by the fact that it was ski season, and almost all flights were booked full. Finding an empty seat for someone on a subsequent flight was seldom an option.

It was after seven p.m., and Patty had just about put all the pieces of the broken schedule back together again. One of the final pieces was Flight 217, and it had finally departed Steamboat. There were several connecting passengers on the delayed flight, and Patty had found seats for Carol Vittone to Chicago, and Jeff and Luann Mercer to Orlando. Jon Pratt's flight to Gillete, Wyoming was in serious doubt due to limited options. The schedule that was on Patty's mind now was her own. She anticipated being in her coat with purse in hand by eight p.m. and ready to do battle with the icy roads on her drive home. That happy thought disappeared at seven-thirty when she was informed that Flight 217 was returning to Steamboat. Patty would not need her coat or purse until the next day.

Patty recalls, "We began looking at the schedule for the remainder of the evening and also for the next morning in case our airplane was RON (remain overnight) in Steamboat. A few minutes later my boss, Dennis Heap, came in with even worse news. He told me the flight was overdue and possibly down. He asked that I pull all the passenger records and find as much contact information as possible. We hoped and prayed for the best, but it was soon apparent that we had lost an aircraft. I asked a few of our employees to stay past their shift and help with the workload. We were a small airline and our coworkers were like an extended family. Everyone was cross trained to perform duties beyond their job description, and we simply did what was necessary to make the airline a success. Everyone was concerned about who the crew was. We soon learned that Scott and Gary were flying the airplane.

"It was our responsibility to contact as many of our passengers' families as possible and inform them of the situation. Dennis and I began making the calls. We told them as much information as we knew and provided them with phone numbers they could call to stay in touch with us. We assured them that all resources were being brought to bear, and we promised to call them with any new information as soon as we knew more. There was a flurry of activity at first, but then all we knew was that search and rescue teams were actively searching. We tried to call each family once an hour or so even if we didn't have new information. We also began making contingency plans for operating the airline with one less airplane."

*****

Vern Bell was still dizzy and standing outside the airplane. He recalls, "I saw Jon Pratt near the tail of the airplane and I struggled through the waist deep snow to reach him. I introduced myself and Jon asked me to help him get into the baggage compartment to see if we could get extra clothes for everyone and find something to plug the holes in the cabin. We got the door open, and Jon crawled inside to open suitcases. I gave him my knife to cut into the ones that were locked, and he passed clothes out so I could give them to people in the cabin. We plugged the openings in the fuselage with suitcases, clothes, and as I recall, one of the passenger's wedding dress. Another passenger by the name of Dave was able to help for a while also, but his back was in extreme pain, and he wasn't able to go too long. Nonetheless, he was helpful.

"Inside the cabin there was a lot of moaning and groaning with all the injuries. I believe some of the people were unconscious for quite a while as well. One of the passengers thrashed around at times throughout the night due to his injuries. I remember at one point, we checked on the other passengers to see how they were doing. I checked on a lady I had been sitting near and she was unconscious. I couldn't find a pulse. If I recall correctly, she was traveling with two other friends."

*****

The CAP ground search team was making progress. Dan Alsum said, "Soon after we passed Idaho Springs, the snowfall increased and the highway became obscured and packed with heavy snow. Once we passed the Berthoud Pass exit, it was impossible to see the pavement at all."

Jerry Alsum added, "I remember as we were driving up Interstate-Seventy we could hardly see where the edge of the road was, so we used our spotlights to light up the reflector posts and guard rails alongside the highway since it had not been plowed. Progress was slow and we were the only ones on the road, so speed was only about fifteen to thirty miles an hour all the way to Kremmling."

Harry Blakeman remembered the drive. "After the briefing in the Safeway parking lot, we headed west on Interstate-Seventy. It was windy with some old snow blowing around, but just a few miles up the interstate snow started falling and steadily increased as we headed toward the Eisenhower Tunnel. By the time we got to Georgetown, it was snowing hard, and the wind was increasing again. I knew when there were high winds like that, it was extremely treacherous on the interstate adjacent to Georgetown Reservoir. Over the years, I had seen many cars with their windows blown out and pickups with campers blown off along that short stretch of I-70. We could go in the snow, but visibility and braking were poor. We proceeded very carefully with good spacing between vehicles to avoid a mishap."

Once the slow moving convoy reached Silverthorne, they were forced to leave the comfort of the interstate and head north on Highway Nine. The conditions only became worse.

Don Niekerk said, "On Highway Nine, between Silverthorne and Kremmling, as we were driving by Green Mountain Reservoir, we picked up the ELT signal and it pointed to Buffalo Pass."

Harry added, "My vehicle-mounted emergency locator receiver featured a high gain antenna and a pre-amp which allowed it to pick up weak signals, and I began hearing the ELT as we passed the Green Mountain Reservoir. About ten miles south of Kremmling, we started hearing the signal consistently. We stopped on the roadway to do direction finding, hoping no one came along and plowed into us. There was too much snow to pull off the road. I remember barely being able to stand on the ice coated highway with the wind blowing very hard. Snow was blowing in my eyes and accumulating on the direction finder box. We received the signal on the handheld direction finders also, and it was pointing in the general direction of Muddy Pass, but we could not be sure that was accurate. We were near the power generating plant at the north end of Green Mountain Reservoir, and realized it was possible the ELT signal was being radiated by the power transmission lines. The ELT signal might be traveling along the power lines instead of directly to our receiver. I had experienced this quite a few times although not for a great distance.

"Our convoy continued on to Kremmling where we found the bar and restaurant at the old hotel still open. We were well aware that time was precious and we needed to get to Flight 217 as rapidly as possible, but it was the last spot where we could stop to check maps, update information, and have access to a telephone. The lady at the hotel was very pleasant and grateful that we were out in the middle of the storm searching for Flight 217. She made sandwiches and coffee for us to take along. Sonny got on the phone with Earl Berger and then briefed us. Some circuit breakers on the power line had tripped about the same time the aircraft would have gone down. This was unusual on a high voltage power line where squirrels don't climb up and short out the lines or tree limbs don't fall and short out the lines. Also, someone driving on State Route Fourteen had reported seeing red and green aircraft position lights. The power line clue indicated that the missing aircraft had struck the transmission line, but exactly where?

"We also had clues from the radio transmission from Flight 217 at 7:40 p.m. They reported being on the Victor 101 Airway crossing the 335-degree radial of Kremmling VOR. That was the last transmission that for sure came from Flight 217. We were thinking about how busy the crew must have been trying to manage their aircraft and the emergency. So if they were too busy to answer the radio, how far could they have flown from the point they reported to Denver Center?"

Jerry Alsum said, "Once we got to Kremmling, we found an open restaurant and looked over the map to formulate a plan. We were picking up the ELT signal in Kremmling too, and it pointed us toward the Rabbit Ears Pass area east of Steamboat. We planned to continue on Route Forty until we got to Route Fourteen, which went north toward Walden."

As mission coordinator, Sonny Elgin was putting the pieces together to form the big picture and evaluate the resources available to him.

"Upon reaching Kremmling, we stopped at the only place in town that was still open—the local bar. I placed a phone call to Earl Berger, back in the Denver area, to get an update. He reported that an Air Force C-130 aircraft had picked up an emergency locator transmitter (ELT) signal, and that there had been a momentary loss of power on the transmission line going over Buffalo Pass east of Steamboat Springs. I immediately suspected that the flicker in power could have been from the aircraft striking the power line somewhere along its course over the pass. I related this info to the other searchers, and we proceeded in the direction of Buffalo Pass. The lady who ran the bar had made coffee and sandwiches for us to take along.

"A few miles west of Kremmling, the snow had let up a little, and our convoy stopped to allow those with direction finding (DF) equipment to check for a signal. They were receiving an ELT signal but could not get a good direction on the target. As we continued north on Highway Forty, the snow began to get heavier again. By the time we got to the Colorado Highway Fourteen turnoff, the snow was very heavy. Jim Alsum was driving the lead vehicle. He was pulling the rescue trailer and was starting to have difficulty with the bumper deep snow. I moved to the lead position and broke trail as we continued north."

*****

Jon Pratt and Vern Bell continued searching the baggage compartment for anything that might be of use. Reality had set in and there was nowhere to turn for help. They *were* the help. Their injuries were not exactly minor but far less than most of the other passengers, and they set about doing what they could for themselves and everyone else.

Jon said, "As we worked through the luggage, I found some athletic socks and put them on Vern's hands to serve as gloves—not ideal, but better than nothing. I couldn't see what was on his feet, but I found no footwear in the luggage to offer him. A few bags were locked, and the small pocket knife I had was not very useful cutting the side of a plastic suitcase. Vern produced a larger pocket knife, and I was able to get in all the bags.

"Along the way, I found a pair of unknown passenger's jeans and slipped them on over the ones I was wearing for additional warmth. When we finished sifting through the luggage, Vern and I were standing beside the main door with all the empty luggage spread across the snow. Vern was commenting more than complaining about how cold his feet and hands were.

"Then the woman I had been sitting next to climbed out of the main cabin door and managed a couple of steps toward us. She was clearly in shock as she asked, 'Are the pilots all right? Has anyone checked on the pilots? Does the radio work? We aren't going to slide down the hill are we?' Three times in a row, the same questions without waiting for an answer. Then she asked a few more times, just repeating, 'We aren't going to slide down the hill are we?' She was wearing a light sweater and had her hands stuffed in her pockets. I couldn't see her shoes, but I imagined they were not the same heavy hiking boots I was wearing.

"She seemed so small, almost frail there in a blizzard, in the middle of an endless snowfield, bewildered. I walked up to her and grabbed her by the shoulders and asked, 'what is your name?'"

"Carol."

"Listen Carol, we've been in a plane wreck in the mountains, do you understand?"

Without expression or emotion, she replied, "Okay."

"I'll check on the pilots in a little bit. I don't know if the radio works or even where to find it, and no, we are not going to slide down the mountain."

Jon was still holding her shoulders and asked, "Do you understand me…do you understand?"

She managed a weak, "Yes."

Jon asked, "Do you know where we are?"

With a blank expression she parroted his previous words, "We are in the mountains in a plane wreck."

Jon said, "I was not certain she was fully coherent yet and asked where she was from. I got a simple reply, 'Chicago.' I was taken aback by what this city girl must be thinking. A city girl suddenly thrust into the most horrific situation imaginable.

"In an attempt to provide something for her to hold onto, I said, 'Listen Carol, I grew up in the mountains and I know a lot about survival in the mountains—we are going to be all right. Now, get back into the plane and help some of the people who are hurt if you can. Do you have any warmer clothes with you? Put on every piece of clothing you have, and tell the others to do the same.'"

"I walked her to the door and helped her back inside. I slowly lowered myself into the door after her and was confronted with anyone's worst nightmare.

"What I saw, and more importantly heard, was overwhelming. I knew the ABCs of first aid—airway—breathing—circulation, and the basic survival skill priorities—heat—shelter—water, but all the survival skills and first aid training in the world were not going to be adequate tonight. This was a mass triage situation which I was not prepared for, but for some reason, I felt responsible to do the best I could. It appeared I was the only person focused on the big picture and not on themselves or a loved one. It felt like a really bad nightmare—one on twenty, try to save them all.

"I tried to blot out all the noise, but before I could formulate a plan, the woman who helped open the door, Cathy Williams, was begging me with tears in her eyes, to help her friend. They had been seated in the very back of the cabin, and there was a man half sitting and half leaning on her friend. He was slowly massaging an oxygen mask with his hands. It was covered in blood, and he seemed to be mesmerized by the texture of the mask and the blood. I grabbed the man under the shoulders and could not say if he was heavy or light—I simply pulled him out of the cabin where Vern helped lower him onto the snow.

"With both of us staring at this incoherent and mumbling soul, sitting in the snow among the suitcases, I said, 'There is a huge mess in there. We have to sort through all the people. Let's put all these suitcases back in the baggage compartment to provide some insulation, and we can put people in there. There's a light in the compartment and they will be out of the snow. Soon the temperature will be the same in there as it is in the cabin.'

"We reversed our assembly line with Vern handing me the suitcases. I laid them out on the floor, and with that complete, we lowered the man into the baggage compartment and closed the door. Then Cathy Williams called from the main cabin door, 'It is getting really cold in here, and the snow is coming in. Can we close the door?'

"I asked if Carol could go to the baggage compartment so the man was not alone. Carol climbed out and we helped her into the compartment and closed the door. Vern and I then helped lower the main cabin door as Cathy caught it and latched it shut tight.

"Vern commented again how terribly cold he was and stated he wanted to go inside. He only had one of the socks on his hand now and I said, 'Okay, just one minute.' We walked up to the cockpit, and standing on the wing that was now upside down on the ground, we thought we saw a large glowing light way up the hill in front of the cockpit but couldn't figure out what it might be. We knew that walking very far in the deep snow was not feasible. We discussed if the light could be Golden, Boulder, or perhaps Nederland Colorado. In our minds, all would have been on the flight path. Perhaps we could mount an expedition in the daylight and make our way up the hill.

"We both agreed there would be rescue plans underway as they would certainly know the plane was missing by now. As we moved out in front of the cockpit, we thought we could see some debris. I knew my second bag was loaded in the front baggage compartment, and I thought about making the effort to find it. The bag contained a first aid kit, an emergency road-side travel kit with a couple of small flares, along with more clothes, and my camp stove. I took two steps off the wing of the plane and was nearly waist deep in snow—I turned back. The debris looked so close, but it was not feasible without expending a great deal of energy and becoming soaking wet. Perhaps in the morning daylight.

"The entire side of the cockpit was missing, and when Vern and I peered inside, we could see the pilot was completely exposed. We could tell he was alive as he was breathing in a very raspy breath— almost like a long time smoker's breath. Then we saw the copilot's arm sticking out of the snow. From the elbow up it was just flopping around. Not reaching for anything or trying to dig itself out, just flopping around. I turned away and was almost sick to my stomach. I didn't want to look at it or imagine what was behind it. I was overwhelmed with the enormity of the situation and said a short prayer, 'Oh Lord, please let us be rescued soon.'

"Then I saw a man sitting on the bulkhead that was between the cabin and the cockpit. It was now sideways and he was just sitting there. No noise, no pain and agony like the others, not doing anything to help anyone else. I yelled at him, 'Mister, who are you? Are you the copilot? You! What is your name? Can you help anyone?' He didn't even turn his head. I climbed off the nose of the plane and, Vern said he was freezing again and had to go inside. I told him to go inside and take his tennis shoes off and put on a couple of pair of socks to try to warm up. He headed to the main cabin door at the rear of the fuselage, and I climbed in the emergency exit window at the front of the passenger cabin—noticing the pain on my shin and leg as I lowered myself in. It was not a warm reception.

"People were almost yelling, 'There is no room. Don't step on me. Watch your feet.' I said, 'Guide me in, show me where I can put my feet.' A young woman and a man helped me in. I noticed the lights in the cabin seemed much dimmer. I mentioned this to no one in particular and the general consensus was that they were not getting dimmer. I disagreed, but kept the thought to myself.

"I noticed a man in the front row, still buckled in his seat, but laying on his side now against the plane. He was yelling for his traveling companion, 'Roger... Roger...help me. Roger... Roger, don't leave. Roger... Roger, please help me. Roger... Roger, help me.' Roger was actually standing over his friend, Bob, holding his hand, but Bob was clearly incoherent. It was very unnerving and never ending. I tried to calm the man a bit telling him it was going to be all right and help was on the way. It didn't seem to do anything to calm him. His calling out for Roger did not wane.

65

"I then turned to the young man sitting on the bulkhead. He was wearing a parka like mine and had no visible trauma. Just sitting calmly with a blank stare on his face. I said, 'Mister... Mister, what is your name? Can you help some of these people?' No reply. Still in shock. Another man was just sitting there hunched over and saying, 'Don't touch me. I hurt so much. My back...my back...it hurts so much. Please don't touch me... I can't move.'"

"The young couple on the way to their wedding were lying next to each other, but the groom was kicking about uncontrollably with his cowboy boots. He was kicking his fiancé mercilessly, and she was screaming in agony. Another gentleman was trying to hold on to the groom's legs to keep him from kicking his fiancé who clearly had some severe injuries. The bride was yelling at her fiancé to stop kicking her. Every once in a while, the groom kicked the man holding him and he let out a horrific scream. He had something wrong with his knee and was in great pain himself.

"I wiped my nose and realized it was bleeding and hurt like hell, along with my right eye which was swelling up. It was then I realized my front tooth was hurting like hell also—like an open cavity. I touched my tooth and was greeted with a sharp edge where it had broken off. That accounted for the exposed nerve providing a shooting pain with the cold air.

"Again, I was overwhelmed and wanted to take my sleeping bag and crawl in it where I would be warm. I could last more than a week on my own, especially if I could get to my other bag with my camp stove and pot to melt snow. Was I really the only person to help all these people? Vern was in pretty good shape, but I didn't know if he was helping people in the back of the plane or trying to get warm. All these people were screaming, blood everywhere, crying and pain everywhere—the pilots. Lord help me.

"There was no epiphany or bolt of lightning like a made for TV drama. I just decided to do what I could, the best I knew how. I called for Vern—more like yelled for him. 'Vern, come to the window.' I didn't ask, I just expected him to be there and he was. I grabbed the groom and got him out the window where Vern slid him down the side of the plane to the ground.

"I turned to Roger who was still standing over his friend holding his hand and trying to calm his non-stop cries for help.

'Roger, you need to go to the baggage compartment too. It's sheltered, there's a light in there, and it will be just as warm as here. We need someone to be back there with the injured.' I had turned into a commander. I was barking orders without concern for others. No one else had a plan, so I was going to make one as I went. Roger gingerly stepped over bodies and made it to the window. I grabbed his waist and told Vern to take his arms from the outside, and I lifted him out of the cabin onto the snow. Vern walked him back to the luggage compartment.

*****

Roger Wobbe, a retired Air Force lieutenant colonel, was interviewed by *Air Line Pilot Magazine* reporter C.V. Glines in the April, 1979 issue. Lieutenant Colonel Wobbe "said that he was impressed with the way young Pratt had taken charge of the situation. Although he had a great deal of experience in emergencies during his military career, 'I recognized that this lad knew what he was doing and I quickly decided to follow his orders,'" Wobbe told *Air Line Pilot.* "I had a broken left wrist and a bad gash on my head but was not "out of it." I got into the back end and tried to take care of the man already there who was thrashing around badly.

"'Eventually, three more people were put back there. One of them, another semiconscious man, was put there by Pratt and Bell because he was hurting his fellow passengers, also thrashing about and kicking. A young woman in severe shock also came back but was continually bothered by the two delirious men, so she went back into the main cabin. When Jon shut the baggage door to keep out the blowing snow, the light went out too. Although I could shout to Jon through the bulkhead, I felt very much alone.'"

Chapter 7

Jon continued his attempt to sort people out in the cabin. "I pointed to the comatose man sitting on the bulkhead and said, 'You! You need to go out too. We need to get some room in here.' He stood and stumbled toward me. I didn't notice if he was walking on anyone or if he stepped on Roger's friend who was now calling out non-stop, 'Marcela... Marcela... Oh Marcela help me, please, Marcela help me.'"

"The comatose man spoke as if a child, almost a whisper, 'I really don't think we should go outside.' I said, 'No, you are not going to stay outside, you are going to shelter in the back of the plane. Just down to the luggage compartment. You will be fine there. Now move, we need more room in here. Come on.'"

His response was equally calm and quiet as before, 'I really don't want to go outside. I don't think we should.' Then a gentleman, I think his name was Joe, who seemed very coherent and was trying to calm the bride, said with clear frustration in his voice, 'Come on man, you really need to go. We need more room in here for injured people. Now move!'"

"We were all getting a bit cross and somewhat angry. Again the comatose man said, 'I just don't think we should go outside.' I replied even more firmly, 'You aren't, you're going to the luggage compartment It's just a little way at the end of the plane.' I honestly just wanted to grab him and push him out the window. It was like talking to an insolent child. Finally, the other man yelled at him, 'Come on buddy, get out of here, you've got to go.'"

"Then Vern came to the window and looked in. He and Roger had managed to get the groom into the baggage compartment where Roger, the only coherent person back there, took charge. He took a discarded shampoo bottle and stuck it in the door jamb so the light stayed on in the baggage compartment while the door was closed. I told Vern to grab the comatose man's arms, and I lifted his waist and he was out the window also. Vern walked him back to the baggage compartment.

"I grabbed a dislodged seat and tossed it out the window. I took the injured man's hand who was calling out for Marcela. He was shivering and I said, 'You really need to be quiet. You're driving everyone crazy.' He answered, 'I'm so cold.'"

"I took off my gloves and rubbed his hands—he didn't seem to notice or care. He was still in his seat, on his side now, and he looked content and out of the way in the front corner of the cabin floor, so I decided to move on.

"The bride started crying out, 'My leg...my leg...it's under the seat.' I tried to see what was going on with her leg and when I touched her knee, she screamed in agony. I grabbed another seat and Vern was there at the window to toss it outside. I reached down and was finally able to feel her mangled leg jammed under a seat still attached to the floor. I said, 'I'm going to try to lift this seat a bit, but you will need to pull your leg out when I do. I know it hurts, but you have to pull it out.

"I lifted with all my might and didn't move the seat more than a half inch. I thought I was going to pass out, I was lifting so hard. She didn't move her leg, and when I let the seat back down, she screamed louder than ever.

"I said, 'You didn't move it—you have to pull it out. It's going to hurt, but then it will be better.' The gentleman who had helped me with the comatose passenger chimed in and reinforced what I had said. Again, I reached under the seat and lifted with all my strength, my back taking the strain. I so wanted to break the seat, but it would not give. Then I saw her pull her leg out, and she seemed to gain some relief.

"A woman was sitting quietly holding the baby I had seen board the plane, but she didn't seem to be the infant's mother. They were quiet and calm with no sign of injury. In hind sight, I was doing triage at lightning speed. With relative calm finally in the front of the cabin, aside from the man's insistent calling for Marcela and the occasional cry for Roger, I decided to check the cockpit and see if I could find the radio. I was worried we would lose what little battery power we had left, so I climbed out the window exit and slid to the ground.

"One of my ski buddies who was a pilot had been kidding me about flying 'Rocky Mountain Scareways' as the locals called it and had mentioned the emergency radio frequency a couple of times in jest. I was racking my brain for the emergency number as I climbed up onto the cockpit. The pilot was on the upside and with the side of the cockpit missing, he was exposed to the elements. He was still breathing raggedly, but there was no visible blood. As I cleared the snow around the pilot, I noticed his one arm was terribly mangled and seemed broken in several places. I gingerly stayed clear of his arm as much as possible as I finished clearing the snow. Using Vern's knife, I carefully cut the pilot's seatbelt, worried that I might cut him in the dark. Again, I shouted for Vern to come help me and he magically appeared. I was not sure where he was hanging out, or what he was doing, but he was a God send."

The cockpit was mangled and Vern Bell remembers, "Jon Pratt and I were able to make it to the cockpit to check on the pilot and copilot. Snow was packed around them and had turned to ice. We finally freed the captain and got him out, but the copilot was stuck in tight. We tried to dig him out with our hands and whatever else we could find. We got one of his arms out, but that was about it. Jon stayed up there longer than me since my feet had gone numb in my tennis shoes."

Jon remembers their effort as well. "We pulled the unconscious pilot out of his seat, and I had Vern lower him onto my shoulder. I was standing on the wing which was very slick, and as I stepped off the wing and onto the trail we had created between the emergency exit window and the luggage compartment, I fell under the weight and we crumpled into a heap. Grabbing his shoulders and feet, we managed to get him back to the luggage compartment where we leaned him against the plane. I contemplated how to fabricate a splint for the pilot's bad arm, but realized it was simply not feasible tonight.

"Shelter and keeping everyone as warm as possible was the number one priority tonight. Tomorrow we could work on splints and real first aid. We opened the door to the luggage compartment where Roger squeezed him in. Carol, who had been in the compartment, climbed out and I could see that she was ashen. More shell shocked than when she had first emerged from the crash. She said, 'I can't go back in there.'"

"It was a simple statement. I was afraid we had built a morgue, and she wanted nothing else to do with it. Vern climbed in the back passenger door, and I walked Carol to the emergency exit window where I gave her a boost and she climbed in."

*****

The CAP convoy pushed on to the northwest out of Kremmling, and Harry Blakeman shared his thoughts. "I couldn't help but think of the Wichita State University football team's crash eight years earlier. It was so terrible. I won't go into the gory details, but you just don't forget the sights and the smells of an incident when so many people perish. I kept praying to God there would be survivors in this crash waiting for us to rescue them.

"We stopped at the intersection of Highway Forty and Highway Fourteen to take more direction finding bearings. Unfortunately, there were high voltage power lines near this intersection also and the possibility that the ELT signal was radiating down the line, but we also had a good indication that the signal was coming from the Buffalo Pass area. I believe this is the point where Dave Lindow joined up with us."

Dave Lindow and Ed Duncan had negotiated the icy roads out of Steamboat Springs pulling a flatbed trailer and the snow cat. They traveled south on Highway Forty until it veered east over the mountain range at Rabbit Ears Pass. The pass was so named because it featured two column-like rock formations that appeared very much like a pair of rabbit ears.

Dave said, "We reached the summit at Rabbit Ears Pass about one in the morning and headed down the other side, hoping the lee side of the mountain would protect us from the strong wind and make handling the flatbed easier. We planned to join Highway Fourteen to the north and on to Walden.

"When we finally reached the flatland east of Rabbit Ears Pass and approached the intersection with Route Fourteen, we saw vehicles stopped with people standing outside. We pulled over to see if they needed help and found out they were the CAP search team taking direction finding readings."

Jerry Alsum said, "As we were leaving Highway Forty and heading toward Walden on Route Fourteen, we saw a truck pulling a trailer with a snow cat on it. He pulled over and we asked if he would help us. He said he heard the airplane was missing and was there to assist any way he could. The DF signal was getting stronger and we all headed north."

The search team convoy was growing and they were receiving the ELT signal, but it was now erratic. The direction finder generally indicated they should go to the north west, but the signal was not consistent. In the dark and with the visibility limited by snow, it was hard to see the power lines along the road to determine if they were far enough away to eliminate the interference. Moving slowly, after ten miles or so, they approached the community of Hebron, and noticed the ELT signal seemed to be stronger from the west. They pulled over and got out to extend the antenna to get the best possible signal for the DF receiver. While they were analyzing the signal, another vehicle pulled over and Steve Poulsen and Al Post from Rocky Mountain Rescue introduced themselves. Steve also had extensive training in DF technology and agreed that even though the signal was erratic, it was coming from the west.

Dave Lindow was very familiar with the mountain range east of Steamboat and explained that the power lines crossed the mountain at Buffalo Pass. He also knew that the road going west from Hebron and through Coalmont would carry them into the Routt National Forest and would be the closest access to Buffalo Pass.

Jim Alsum said, "Sonny Elgin, the mission coordinator, was also familiar with the area since his father owned land there. We decided to head toward Buffalo Pass and asked Dave Lindow to lead the way."

The combined force moved slowly west in blowing snow following the flatbed with the snow cat on it, hoping to stay out of the ditch alongside the narrow county road.

*****

Jon Pratt had accomplished about all he could do for the passengers at the moment and decided to return to the cockpit and once again look for the radio.

"As I returned to the cockpit, I was able to pry the captain's seat sideways and move it out of the way. I was surprised it was not more securely attached to the floor and figured it must have broken loose. I then started clearing snow from the instrument panel which was still glowing from some dials. A few sparks popped, but it didn't seem likely I was going to electrocute myself, and at the time it didn't seem important to be careful. I was hoping to find a radio mic and call for help like in the movies, but it was not to be so. The copilot's arm was still sticking out of solid impacted snow that was injected into the cockpit when it took the brunt of the crash and the windscreen, nose cone, doors, and most of the roof were ripped away on impact. The arm wasn't moving anymore and given the density of the snow and ice, it did not seem likely he would have survived. I felt sick that I had left him without aid, but I had felt the need to help the passengers first. They seemed to have the best chance of survival after my initial assessment.

"I continued to dig snow and toss it out of the cockpit for a long time. I just kept working on the snow and clearing the instrument panel. At some point, someone from the cabin handed me a cigarette lighter that I was using for light occasionally. Then I realized we were going to need the lighter tomorrow to start a fire, and I shouldn't be wasting it for light, so I stopped and just kept working from feel. I was about to give up on finding the radio as I was cold and wet and it seemed futile at that point.

"Then the copilots hand next to my knee moved. More slowly now, but it was moving. I started frantically clawing at the impacted snow with nothing but my hands—down the arm to the shoulder working strictly from feel. It was slow going and I couldn't see. It was cramped in the tight space, with mangled portions of the main cabin sticking into the cockpit, as I worked my way deeper into the wreckage. Bent metal kept snagging my coat as I tried to get the snow not only off the copilot but also out of the cockpit. I continued for what seemed like a very long time, digging down his arm, a small trench not bigger than my hand. I was punching the snow as it came out in chunks, not powdered, but closer to ice.

"Down to his shoulder, along the shoulder toward his head, I couldn't see anything in the trench, working by feel alone, I was clawing at the side of his head and ear now. I was merciless with no regard of hurting him, only one thing mattered… *Air!*

"It had been a long time since the crash. I had no idea how long, but I could not believe he could possibly be alive. I knew an avalanche victim only had an hour or so at most to survive after being entombed in packed snow and ice, but it had been several hours. Clawing and scratching furiously, I was in front of his face now and suddenly I heard him take the largest gasp of air ever. He was alive!

"A few more handfuls of snow and I sat back and took a breath of my own. I was exhausted. My gloves and pants were completely soaked and I gave a brief laugh. I don't know why...stress I suppose, or the sense of finally accomplishing something. The problems just kept coming at me, but this one I thwarted. The next problem was hypothermia. Impacted in snow for several hours and the copilot would surely succumb to the cold and wet. Drowsiness, loss of coordination, confusion accompanied by uncontrollable shivering which eventually stops just before death. I knew hypothermia was the enemy for all of us now as the temperatures were dropping. Now I was soaking wet and exhausted, both of which accelerated hypothermia.

"Back to digging out the copilot. I worked down his side and leg that was up because he was lying on his right side. I got most of one leg freed up and expanded the trench around his arm, upper body, and face. Cutting his seat belt off, I tried to lift him straight up by his waist band. He was still half buried and I had to lift a grown man straight up. A bit more digging and another attempt.

"I kept at it, trying to figure out what was holding him in as the lights in the cabin and the instrument panel finally went out completely. I called for Vern to try to help lift him and we both got in and pulled as hard as we could—one on his arm and the other on the waist of his pants. We talked about what could be holding him in and pinning him down. We just couldn't see and I said, 'We've got to get him out of there or he'll die overnight. He'll never last the night with the cold, and he's wetter than I am.'"

"Vern decided to try and I jumped out and he dug for a while and gave another pull. He climbed down and said, 'I just don't think we can get it in the dark.' I checked my watch, two a.m. and I was spent. We decided it was not happening tonight. Vern and I went back and grabbed a few suitcases still lying on the ground, covered in snow as it had been snowing hard all night. We broke the backs of several large suitcases and climbed up to build a shelter over the cockpit, offering some protection from the elements."

*****

Gary Coleman was in critical condition and extreme danger. Not only were his injuries serious—he was trapped in the cockpit, buried in snow, and could not move. His body temperature continued to decrease and he was in and out of consciousness. Each time his awareness returned, he tried to remember what happened and struggled to free himself from the ice. All he could do was call for help and pray. Gary was familiar with cold weather and snow, and he knew the dangers. He and both his brothers were accomplished skiers and understood all the precautions and emergency procedures for rescuing injured skiers. Gary had never considered that he would someday need to be rescued himself. During periods of consciousness, Gary was not only frustrated that he could not free himself—he was livid that he could not help his passengers as he was trained to do and as his character demanded.

Sometimes the margin between life and death is razor thin, and Gary was certainly balanced on that sharp edge. All the odds were against him, despite the heroic efforts of Jon Pratt and Vern Bell. But sometimes the slightest advantage can be the difference, and Gary had only two small things in his favor. The first was the fact that the extreme cold helped coagulate his blood to slow the bleeding from his many lacerations. The second advantage was the wool pilot's uniform his mom insisted that he wear. In addition to the wool socks and pants, she had bought a black wool uniform sweater for him.

Wool is the only material in the world that is grown by mammals to regulate their body temperature in all weather conditions. It's a breathable fiber and provides instant warmth like no other material. Wool is a great buffer to rain, wind, and snow. In cold temperatures, it wicks moisture from the skin, and at the same time, its insulating quality traps dry air and warmth.

At best, the small advantages might buy Gary some time, but he had been trapped for several hours already. At least the snow was no longer falling on him through the opening in the cockpit.

*****

75

Jon Pratt continued to improvise, "I took another smaller suitcase and broke the back and was amazed that it fit near perfectly as a replacement emergency exit window. I never knew what happened to the real emergency window. Vern must have given it a good toss into the snow when he opened it. As I climbed into the window, I lowered the suitcase in place to seal the snow and wind out. The only light came in the form of a faint greenish glow of the emergency exit sign.

"The gentleman with the injured back was bent over a seat with his head on his hands, still moaning, and he seemed to be in great pain. I asked if there was anything I could do to help. He said, 'Oh, I hurt so much, I think I have some internal injuries. If I could only stretch out, but I hurt so much if I try to move.'"

"I tried to look around for a place to lay him out and asked, 'Where can we fit him?' The lady taking care of the baby, Maureen Redmond, in the most kind and calming voice said, 'He could lie straight back and lean his head right here by me.'"

"From the front I gave him a bear hug and tried to lift him, and he calmly declared that his legs hurt too much. He never screamed like many of the others. He seemed to be aware that it was not productive and remained calm the whole time, but it was obvious to me that he was in excruciating pain. His legs were pinned under a seat I could not see. I said, 'You need to help pull your legs out before we try to lay you back,' and he agreed. He threw an arm around my shoulder and I hugged him again and lifted. He was able to free his legs and I laid him back almost flat. He was jammed between the seats and the wall. I gingerly straightened his legs out, and he said, 'That is much better,' in a tone that relayed his tremendous relief.

"Another gentleman said, 'I hope my head stops bleeding.' I carefully took a step toward him and could just make out his hands holding his head with dark blood all over his hands and face. While going through the luggage, I had pulled a belt from a terry cloth bathrobe and stuffed it in my pocket for just such an occasion. I remembered it now and pulled it out and tied it tight around his head wound as a makeshift pressure bandage.

"Exhausted and no immediate demands to deal with, I asked, 'Where can I sit down?' I received silence and said, 'I really would like to sit down somewhere.' This time, Maureen, the calm, cool, and compassionate woman still holding the baby said, 'Carol, could you slide over a bit and let him sit down?' Carol complied without comment. There was just enough room to squat with my knees up to my chest along the curve where the cabin ceiling transitioned to the wall."

Vern Bell was exhausted also. "We finally decided we had done about all we could in the dark, but there was no way to sleep. We huddled through the night, sang some Christmas carols, and tried to keep everyone's spirits up as much as possible while we waited for dawn. The light was very dim inside the cabin, but there was one little exit light that stayed on through the night."

*****

Dave Lindow and Ed Duncan hauled the snow cat west toward Buffalo Pass with the Civil Air Patrol vehicles following close enough to keep their tail lights in sight. Don Niekerk and Harry Blakeman monitored the ELT signal as best as they could and knew they were getting closer. Chunks of ice would occasionally break free of a truck or trailer and smash the following vehicle. Heaters ran at full blast to combat the frigid temperature, and the wind chill factor plummeted. No one wanted to think about what the weather conditions might be if they had to climb to Buffalo Pass.

They passed near the small town of Coalmont and saw no lights. It was after two in the morning, and the residents were never even aware of their presence as they continued west on the mostly deserted road. Fortunately, the narrow two-lane road had been plowed at some earlier point, but snow continued to fall and was rapidly erasing the work of the highway crew. A few miles later the snowplows had abandoned their effort, but the convoy pushed forward on the unplowed surface—doing a little plowing of their own.

Harry Blakeman said, "The snow was probably eight to twelve inches deep and kept getting deeper and the drifts were even higher. We were having trouble breaking through those drifts. Somehow we had gotten here, all the way from Denver, without ever having to put snow chains on any of the vehicles, but even that wouldn't help now."

After a few more miles, even the appearance of a road was all but gone. The county highway crew did not routinely plow the roads in this area due to the fact that no one normally had reason to travel beyond the base of the mountain in winter.

Through the horizontal snow-flakes, they could see a small sign on the left of the road that announced, *Grizzly Creek Station— Routt National Forest.*

There appeared to be a parking area beyond the sign, and they pulled in to assess the situation. Standing at the edge of the parking area, almost like an afterthought to someone's grand design, there was a small log cabin that the park ranger used in the summer months to manage the Grizzly Creek Campground. The entire structure was no more than twenty feet long and fifteen feet wide, but the feature that caught everyone's attention was the chimney on top—shelter and heat.

Photo by Harrison Jones

Grizzly Creek Ranger Station October 2016

They checked the DF receiver and although it was erratic, it directed them toward the deep snow where a road should have been. Dave Lindow had only been on the east side of Buffalo Pass a few times, but he knew the road was there—it was just covered in several feet of snow and ice. Four-wheel drive vehicles had served them well but would carry them no further, and the snow was far too deep for the snow mobiles they had brought along. The small group of men stood in the blowing snow and looked west. They knew a mountain was there, but on this night, visibility was measured in feet rather than miles.

They were not the type of men to stand around doing nothing for very long. Dave Lindow and Ed Duncan climbed up on the flatbed and began clearing snow and ice from the snow cat. Once the hold down chains were loosened and removed, Dave crawled into the cab and fired the machine up. As the engine warmed, and the temperature gauge finally began to show movement, he drove it off the trailer, and the metal tracks dug into the snow and ice.

Team leader Jim Alsum had decisions to make and he didn't hesitate. They were as close as they were going to get without the use of the snow cat, and they needed a base camp. The log cabin was locked up tight for the winter, but that didn't stop Jim, Sonny, and Harry from making a forced entry.

Harry said, "While the other team members were preparing the snow machines, we set out to try to get into the cabin. I remember walking around the right side of the building—the snow was probably three to four feet deep or more, and it wasn't easy walking around except right next to the building. The wind had blown the snow away from the side of the building and away from the rear door area. We were able to unlock that rear door without causing any damage. We found some firewood and got a fire started in the stove and then set up the *on scene* command center."

Once inside they found two small rooms, a kitchen, and a sleeping area with bunk beds. There was no running water, but the kitchen was equipped with a propane cooking stove, and the bunkroom had a pot-belly stove for heat.

Sonny said, "Once we were inside the cabin, I got the lights turned on and the heater going. It was a small cabin, but suited our needs at the time."

Jim and Sonny had set up base camps in many locations, and the little cabin was as good as it was going to get for this mission. They were not aware that the tiny structure had a long history. The cabin had actually stood at the Grizzly Creek location since 1922 and had been originally built by Forest Service Ranger, George McClanahan, to house his family while he was in the field. The cabin had served many rangers since, and it would serve the Civil Air Patrol well on the morning of December 5, 1978.

Jim related, "After forcing our way into the cabin, we opened the rescue trailer and took out the portable stove and our water supply for the base camp. We then began loading as much rescue equipment as possible onto Dave's snow cat. We didn't know what they might need to reach the airplane, and we didn't know if there would be survivors. An airplane crash in the mountains usually turned out to be a recovery mission and not a rescue."

Jim knew that every man present—including himself—wanted to continue to the crash site and help any way they could, but he also knew the snow was too deep for snowmobiles, and the snow cat could only carry four men once all the rescue equipment was loaded aboard.

"I had to decide who to send up the mountain with Dave, and I chose my son Jerry because he was an EMT, Don Niekerk because he also had EMT training and operated the DF receiver, and Steve Poulson from Rocky Mountain Rescue because he was experienced with mountain rescue and could communicate what was needed if they found the airplane. I gave Jerry my DF unit, CAP FM radio, and a search and rescue frequency radio. They left the base camp at about three a.m."

Photo Courtesy of Dave Lindow

Dave Lindow's snow cat

Dave Lindow learned about the crash when he saw the evening news in Steamboat Springs. He immediately went to the Routt County Sheriff and volunteered himself and the snow cat for the search and rescue effort. Dave and Ed Duncan loaded the snow cat on a flatbed trailer and hauled it over Rabbit Ears Pass, in blizzard conditions, in order to reach the search area. Dave, along with Jerry Alsum, Don Niekerk, and Steve Poulson were the first to arrive at the crash site. Other snow cats eventually arrived to help evacuate the survivors, but Dave had the only fully enclosed snow cat. The others had open beds like a pickup truck.

Chapter 8

Don Coleman and Ron Plunkett were still fighting the blizzard and the icy roads out of Denver. Ron said, "We stopped at Don's condo in Dillion so he could pick up his winter gear. It was about three a.m. and I called my CAP contact again to get the latest news. Our Grand Lake neighbor, Bill Ayers, was on duty with CAP the evening of the crash. I told him that Gary had a personal ELT with him, and he immediately interrupted me and told me they'd had multiple echoes. He thought a second ELT might explain that and help confirm the location.

He was monitoring all the CAP communications and explained the location of the power lines and told us the search and rescue team had set up a base camp at the Grizzly Creek Ranger Station. We hit the road again and drove the rest of the night through Kremmling and headed to Grizzly Creek."

*****

Colorado State Patrol Sgt. Jack Donner arrived in Walden to find quite a few volunteers had gathered with snowmobiles and other equipment to aid in the search. It had been discovered that a power outage had occurred at about the time the airplane went down, and speculation was, the two events might be related.

Jack explained, "We decided to begin the search by investigating the high voltage power lines that crossed the county. That was a lot of miles of power lines, and when we got the word that Civil Air Patrol had narrowed their search to the Grizzly Creek area, we were in a totally different part of the county.

"I headed down Highway-Fourteen and made the turn-off toward Grizzly. I got as far as Coalmont before the road became impassable for my cruiser. There was a highway barn outside Coalmont where the county kept some of their road equipment, and we gathered there and spread maps out on the hood of the car to see how the power lines crossed the area. The CAP folks explained that their tracking equipment indicated the crash was probably in the Buffalo Pass area. That was not good news in that Buffalo Pass would be hard to reach in the blizzard conditions we were experiencing. The Grand County Coroner called in four-wheel-drive ambulances to standby for possible survivors, and I left the cruiser in Coalmont and rode one of the ambulances on to Grizzly Ranger Station. The ambulance had a radio so I could stay in touch with Hot Sulphur Springs, and after I got to Grizzly, the CAP guys had good radios too.

"I discovered that Sheriff Swayze had not arrived, so by default I became in charge of the scene. Later, I found out that the sheriff and one of his part time deputies were searching a different part of the county and were out of radio contact. More and more people began to arrive, but the organization was good and security was not a problem. I was able to keep the dispatcher at Hot Sulphur Springs informed as to the progress of the search and what was needed at the scene. We were very fortunate that snow cats were available to go up the mountain. It would have been difficult and much more time consuming to make that trip on a snowmobile. It seemed that everyone brought water with them, but nobody brought food. My wife, Lonnie, worked at the *Country Cupboard Café* in Kremmling and in hindsight, I should have asked the owner, Ardis Wright, to send food to the scene. Ardis was always a big supporter of law enforcement, and I'm sure she would have donated food and beverage. In fact, I found out later that the Civil Air Patrol Team had stopped in Kremmling earlier in the evening, and Ardis had fixed coffee and sandwiches for them to take along."

*****

Putting four men in the cab of the snow cat was a tight squeeze and far less than comfortable considering they had filled most of the space with rescue equipment. They were not small men, and they were layered with enough winter garb to open a small department store. But that was the least of Dave Lindow's problems. The deep snow and limited visibility made it impossible to actually follow the road. If there appeared to be an opening between the trees, he could only assume that meant there was a road.

To complicate matters further, there were many logging roads that intersected the forest service road that wound its way to the top of the mountain. The logging trails usually extended into the forest for a short distance and then ended abruptly at a dead end—making it necessary to backtrack and explore a different direction. The snow was deep and there was no way to know what was beneath it—fallen trees, huge rocks, tree stumps…all made for a bumpy ride. Dave nonetheless pushed on—forging a trail up the mountain. In addition, the antenna of the DF unit could not be extended inside the cab, making it necessary to stop often and get out to analyze the signal.

Don Niekerk and Jerry Alsum were well aware of the fact that using a direction finding unit involved art as well as science. There was no magic needle that simply pointed to the target. In 1978, emergency locator technology was still evolving, and the state of the art was transistor radio receivers. One must first understand the science in order to utilize the art of interpreting the signal.

The ELT transmitter installed on the airplane was not a high powered device due to the fact that it utilized a self-contained battery as a power source and the stronger the signal, the less battery life available. In fact, the transmitter used less than one watt of electrical power. That is minuscule compared to many normal AM broadcast news and music stations that utilize as much as 50,000 watts of power.

Secondly, in order to be useful, the signal had to be broadcast on a frequency that could be received by search aircraft. The normal band for aviation communications is VHF (very high frequency) and that requires a line of sight signal. Simply put, the signal can be compared to a flashlight. The beam of light is very useful as long as there is no obstacle between the flashlight (the transmitter) and the object being illuminated (the receiver). In theory, the ELT was very effective if received by a high flying aircraft. There are generally no obstacles in the sky between the transmitter and the aircraft receiver, and the system was effective up to 200 miles. However, it was far more challenging for a search and rescue team in a snow cat at ground level.

There were many obstacles between the snow cat and the ELT, including trees, hills, rocks, and possibly the airplane wreckage itself. In addition to that, the airplane was located beneath a high power transmission line that carried 230,000 volts of electricity, creating a magnetic field to distort the ELT signal and carry it along the wires instead of in a straight line. Another factor involved the possibility of Gary Coleman's personal ELT transmitting a simultaneous overlapping signal.

84

The DF receiver itself presented two elements to analyze. It received an audio signal as well as a signal to interpret for direction. The audio signal simply got louder as you moved closer to the transmitter. The handheld DF units that Don Niekerk and Jerry Alsum used were manufactured by L-Tronics and commonly known as the L-Per. The box itself was truly handheld at only 4.5" X 3.5". The antenna; however, was a little more involved and featured a wooden mast with a cross arm and four metal rods that unfolded to deploy for reception.

Photo courtesy of Don Niekerk

Jim Alsum demonstrates the use of the L-Per direction finding unit used in the search for Flight 217. Jim was involved in more than 300 search and rescue missions over a span of thirty-two years. He served Civil Air Patrol as emergency services director, mission pilot, and counter drug officer.

Harry Blakeman described the operation of the L-Per. "The process involved rotating the antenna until the strength indication peaked on the small meter and then proceeding in that direction. The DF mode gave an indication to either the left or the right on the meter.

If everything was working correctly, when the antenna was rotated and the meter was centered, that meant you were directly facing the source of the ELT signal. However, the DF unit could not give an indication of distance to the ELT. That information could only be determined by taking bearings from two locations and drawing those lines on a map to see where they intersect."

The audio signal sounded like a cheap or broken siren. Normally the sound produced by a siren starts low and ascends to a higher tone, then descends back down. The ELT audio only used the descending half of the siren cycle. It always starts high and descends, rapidly repeating the urgent sound.

The direction finding unit presented many challenges for the search team as they ascended the mountain. The audio signal told them they were getting closer, but going left or right was not always an option without falling off a downslope or into a chasm.

As technology improved in later years, ELTs would become much easier to track. Batteries would become much more efficient as a power source, and the ELT would be capable of transmitting on several frequencies rather than just one. Eventually ELTs could be received by satellites and actually transmit the latitude and longitude of their exact location. In 1978, that technology was still many years away. Jerry Alsum and Don Niekerk worked with the equipment available at the time.

Dave Lindow downplayed what would seem almost impossible to those less experienced. "I was not as familiar with the east side of Buffalo Pass but didn't have any real problems traveling up the mountain. The heavy snow and wind restricted the visibility to almost nothing in some places, and the logging roads were a nuisance, but we made steady progress."

Jerry Alsum described the experience, "Once we got to the Grizzly Creek Campground, Dad and Sonny decided it was time to stop driving and use the snow cat. Dad decided to send a three-man team up the mountain with Dave Lindow. He decided I would go because I was an EMT, and he chose Don Niekerk because he was in EMT training at the time, and Steve Poulsen from Rocky Mountain Rescue. We loaded the snow cat with as much gear as we could. We took first aid supplies, blankets, sleeping bags, shovels etc. There was barely enough room for the four of us.

"As we were driving into the forest, Dave told us that he was somewhat familiar with the pass and knew the power lines crossed the road in a couple of places. We felt the power lines would be the best shot at finding the plane because of the power outage experienced in Walden about the time the air traffic controller lost contact with the flight. I asked Dave to stop at the point where the power lines first crossed over the road, and we would take our first DF reading at that location.

"As we were going along, we would go up the road and then Dave would stop and say, 'No, this isn't right. This is a logging road.' We just reversed back out of that road and tried a different direction. While we called them roads, you couldn't really see them as roads, just spaces through the forest where no trees existed. I estimated the snow to be between four and six feet deep. I remember thinking we might find a horrific scene based on other crashes we had found. Bodies torn up, planes that were no longer recognizable as planes, wreckage scattered for hundreds of feet.

"We finally got to a point where Dave said the power lines were overhead even though it was snowing so hard we couldn't possibly see them from inside the snow cat. Once we got out, we could see the lines directly over us, and we took a DF reading. It was very confusing—the DF unit would show one direction, and then a couple of seconds later, it would show a different direction. It became a challenge to decide which way the reading pointed us."

Don Niekerk remembered the experience as well. "Once we reached the Grizzly Ranger Station. It was decided that Jerry Alsum, Steve Poulson, and I would go on the rescue team with Dave Lindow in the snow cat. Jerry used his dad's DF radio and I had mine. We brought both DF radios with us because the power lines were causing interference with the ELT signal from the airplane. We stopped many times so Jerry and I could get out and take DF readings. We compared the readings on both units because the power lines made it hard to get a definite direction.

"I remember jumping out of the snow cat, and the snow came up to my chest. We were told later that with the wind blowing so hard, the wind chill that night was probably between twenty-five and fifty degrees below zero. The distance from the base camp to the top of Buffalo Pass was about thirteen miles."

Jerry Alsum added, "I asked Dave if the power lines crossed the road anywhere else, and he said they crossed at the top. We worked our way up the mountain and finally reached the top at Buffalo Pass. We had learned that when we jumped off the snow cat, we would be in snow at least up to our waist. The DF signals were still erratic and inconsistent, but we took more readings at different locations. I remember thinking to myself *this is crazy.* We were going to need more people to find the airplane. There was so much area to cover—it was going to be hard to pinpoint the plane's location. The signal was very strong, so we knew we were at least getting closer."

*****

Jon Pratt was physically and mentally exhausted. He had physically exerted himself for hours now inside and outside the airplane, and his mind continued to call on all his experience for answers to one problem after another. His Eagle Scout training gave him the confidence to know that he would survive, but the same training made him feel responsible for twenty-one other desperate souls on Buffalo Pass. Ironically, neither Jon nor anyone else knew exactly where the airplane was located.

"Sleep was hard to come by, with both pair of jeans and my boots soaked. My legs cramped and were numb from lack of circulation. My hands were freezing, and I took my gloves off, rubbing them together and putting them inside my coat. I couldn't stretch out without putting my feet on top of an injured lady who had not regained consciousness. I think she was the baby's mom, Margie Kotts, lying in front of me in the dark. She had been lying there since the crash with neither a moan, or a groan nor any sound at all. I could tell that she was breathing, but that was it.

"The man up front was still at it, calling out for his loved ones, although much less frequently now. The baby would cry occasionally and Maureen would calm him down. Other moans and groans could be heard all night from those who were conscious. A man in the back occasionally would call out, 'Oh Lord, help us, please save us,' and repeat it a while later. The unconscious would join in at random times with a groan and the occasional semi-conscious call for help. If anyone tried to move, someone else was affected, and the offender would receive a cry of pain or scolding.

"Whenever the baby cried or someone called out in pain, the man up front would say, 'Hey, let's hold it down, some of us are trying to sleep.' Given the situation, it seemed rather funny as he was making the most noise of anyone. Rocking and crying out almost all night long.

"I was exhausted and needed to try and get some rest. I noticed my sleeping bag was covering three people including Carol next to me. I so wanted to get in the sleeping bag and get warm, but I figured they needed it more. I said the Lord's Prayer to myself softly and closed my eyes and tried to ignore my numb legs and toes.

"My thoughts were running wild as I sat there, wondering what tomorrow would bring, and I started to make a plan. I had not returned to the back of the cabin, and I vowed to check on them first thing in the morning along with the baggage compartment folks. I decided I would first try to get a fire started and then try to make it to where I thought the nose cone luggage was scattered. People were cold, but with all the bodies in the cabin, and it sealed up quite well, I didn't feel the cold would kill us. I was thinking of how to make water and keep us hydrated. I knew lack of hydration accelerated the onset of hypothermia. Exhausted, I must have caught some sleep.

"The copilot woke up around four a.m. and started yelling for someone to help him. He kept saying, 'Help me I'm stuck. I'm almost out. Can you please help me?' On and on he repeated his cries for help, getting louder with each plea. 'I'm almost out, can you see me? Come and help, please!'"

"I said, 'We'll get you out in the morning—we can't see now.' I asked, 'Where are we?' He rambled off some numbers and then Kremmling. All I understood was the name of the town of Kremmling. It made no sense we were near Kremmling. I believed we were much closer to Denver. Kremmling was near our departure at Steamboat Springs. I figured he was just confused since we would have flown over Kremmling early in the flight. I felt everyone was staring at me and wondering why I didn't get up and help the copilot. He was so convincing that he could get out with a little help. I feigned sleep, so no one asked for any more help.

"A few passengers were praying, and I heard a few soft hymns coming from somewhere in the dark. Around five-thirty a.m. Maureen, who was still caring for the baby, asked the time and I told her. She commented, 'Oh, it will be light soon and maybe we can see something.' This started a debate over when it would be light. I said, 'It's almost the shortest day of the year, it won't be really light till near seven a.m.' She disagreed and was sure it would be light much sooner. Then someone else gave their opinion. I gave in. It didn't matter. It would be light when it was light...and we would still be here."

*****

Maureen Redmond wondered if the night would ever end. She had been huddled in the freezing floor of the cabin for over eight hours caring for Matt and doing what she could for Margie and others.

"The folks who were able to move about put the thrashing people in the luggage space, and someone sat back there all night and held them down as best they could. I don't know who that was, but he must have thought he was in hell.

"As the night wore on, someone realized we were under power lines, but I couldn't begin to guess where since I didn't know we had turned around. I think Jon finally figured it out and was talking about trying to ski down the mountain and follow the power lines to look for help. They talked about how long we might be stranded and the steps we should take.

"I don't think I talked much. I just felt like I was in a daze. We could hear the copilot crying out all night, 'Help me! Help me! Get me out!' I know Jon Pratt and Vern Bell tried to dig him out, but he was totally encased in snow and ice. I remember wishing he would just realize there was nothing we could do and stop calling out. It was so terrible to know he was in such bad shape. I remember some saying to him over and over, 'We'll get you out. You'll be okay.' That seemed to me not to be true, but maybe it helped him. I felt sure he would not survive.

"Sometime during the night someone in the back called out, 'Hey, I think this lady has passed away.' We were horrified and shouted, 'Shut up,' but it was true, and it was my friend, Mary Kay.

She never regained consciousness. I tried to pretend that it wasn't true.

"I was thinking when morning came and the sun came out, we could make sense of things. As it got closer and closer to dawn, I realized the sun was not going to come out and the storm was continuing. We could all freeze to death if we had to spend another night there."

*****

Dave Lindow had been maneuvering the snow cat continuously for over two hours, and everyone on the search team had been awake for almost twenty-four hours. They had not had much to eat or drink although they made sure to bring water, and Dave was wise enough to have a thermos of hot coffee in the snow cat. The temperature was colder than it had been all night. The snow was coming down like it would never stop, and the wind was approaching hurricane force at the top of the pass where the altitude was almost 11,000 feet above sea level. Dave was an experienced pilot and glad he was in the snow cat and not an airplane as the mountain wave continued to pummel the crest of Buffalo Pass.

They were hours away from civilization and totally dependent on the snow cat. If the machine threw a track, or the engine failed for some reason, or if they tipped over on one of the many steep inclines they had encountered, their own survival could be a problem. No one brought the subject up. They were all too tired to worry about it.

Dave remembered reaching the summit. "It had taken about an hour to ascend the east side since it was quite hard to tell which road was the correct one. I had never been on, nor up, the east side in the winter, but through trial and error, we made it. Once there, it was not hard to tell as the terrain flattened out and visibility basically disappeared. Windshield wipers were useless, and actually it was blowing so hard the snow wound up not sticking to the windshield—it just blew off.

"On the way up, I had discussed my thoughts as to the power line circuit breaker popping, the strong yet usually unfelt downdrafts on the east side with high upper-level winds, and the fact that the sectional chart showed the V101 airway intersecting the power lines

91

just east of the top. To me it was clear where to start, but at the top, everyone else put their hopes and faith on the DF signals. I felt they were leading us in erroneous directions as every time we stopped, the box pointed somewhere else. I assumed it was interference from the power line's magnetic field, and we were just wasting time.

"Anyway, we wound up chasing the signals north, then south, and even west which was downhill to into the upper Fish Creek drainage close by the power line. After proceeding a ways down-hill to the west, I stopped and said if we continued further we would not be able to get back uphill and would need rescuing ourselves. My previous explorations of that drainage area for good powder skiing terrain in the past had led to several times where we couldn't climb back up the slope we had just came down and thus having to back out via another route. Hard to do in good visibility—at night in a snowstorm—impossible.

"Fortunately, the trees at the top run in occasionally interrupted strips parallel to the divide and perpendicular to the westerly winds. This made it possible for me to orient myself and know which way—north or south—I was going. Having a compass back then during previous explorations had never crossed my mind since visibility was always good. We just kept the trees on our right going south or on the left going north. Visibility in the lee of the trees was actually quite good and when the trees stopped and visibility went to zero, I just held the wheel until we got behind the next band of trees. It was like flying on instruments, except we were on the ground. Spooky feeling.

"It was easy to tell when we were under the power lines. We couldn't see them, but the crackling sound they made was audible even in the cab. Our excursions at the top led us probably a quarter mile north of the road to a half-mile south of the power lines. Maybe a mile and a half overall. Lots of time was spent trying to get a signal which pointed in the same direction as the last. That pretty much ate up the time between four a.m. until five-thirty.

"As with anyone who had learned to fly in Colorado, I was quite familiar with the different parameters of mountain flying. I knew the local terrain and weather patterns well, especially along the common routes in and out of Steamboat Springs. I just had an intense feeling that with the powerline circuit breaker tripping, the smooth yet intense downdrafts we found on the east side of the pass, and the fact that the V-101 airway intersected both of them slightly east of the top, that we would find the airplane just by following the powerlines downhill to the east. I knew the west side and top of Buffalo Pass like the back of my hand, but my experience on the east side was limited. Nonetheless, I decided we should explore that direction."

Jerry Alsum and Don Niekerk had never experienced such crazy DF signals. Jerry said, "Dave decided that we should just try to track the powerlines down the mountain and see how far we could make it. We decided to head that direction even though there was no road at all. We were directly under the power lines, and the path started going downhill gently, and that was fine until we came to a point where the hill became rather steep. I began to question whether the snow cat would be able to get back up that hill if we went down it. I suggested to Dave that we stop and take one more reading to make sure we were going in the right direction."

*****

Jon Pratt couldn't rest, and he couldn't sleep with so many people suffering. "I anxiously waited for daylight, which we all felt would bring hope and an opportunity to help more people. Maybe we could organize the passenger cabin and make everyone a bit more comfortable. I was peering at the crack between my makeshift suitcase window, and I could see it was still dark at six a.m.

"I thought I might have heard something, but my mind had been playing tricks on me all night with both light and sound. But then I heard it more certainly now.

"I said, 'Shut up…everyone shut up. I think I hear something.'

"Everyone grew quiet and I repeated, 'I think I hear some machines.'"

Maureen said, "Yes, so do I."

"My heart raced as I knocked the suitcase in the emergency exit window out of the way. A good four inches of snow fell in on everyone, which surprised me. Most of it fell on Maureen, who was just below the emergency exit.

"I climbed out the window and saw two large headlights pointing at us through the darkness a way off. A car, a bus, a snow plow? What was it?

"Then I saw the blue lights on top of it and recognized it as a snow cat. I saw a person walk in front of the headlights and I screamed, 'We're here! We're here!'

"After what seemed like a long silence, someone hollered, 'We see you! We're coming! We have to drive around these trees.'"

"I could see there were a lot of trees between the snow cat and me. I screamed as loud as I could, 'We love you.' I turned back to the window and shouted in, 'We're saved!'"

Maureen Redmond's heart pounded. "It was about six a.m. when Jon shouted he heard a machine and to be quiet. And then we saw lights too. I panicked that they would pass us by, and I handed Matthew to someone and pulled myself through the window thinking I would run and stop them. When I slid down the side of the airplane, I was up to my chest in snow. Of course they were not going to pass us by, and I went back and got Matthew."

*****

Dave said, "We started down the east side of the mountain about five-thirty in the morning. Shortly after getting under the power lines—maybe a quarter of a mile downhill—the DF receiver started squawking even inside the cab with the antenna folded up. We were shocked, yet quite hopeful, so we piled out to see if we could get a reading. I vividly remember standing next to the idling cat with snow blowing past us when suddenly I heard a muffled voice out of the dark that sounded like, 'Over here!' Holy shit may have been uttered next. We all piled back into the cat and drove another few hundred feet under the power line until suddenly a dark figure appeared standing waist deep in the snow waving his arms.

"Jon Pratt came into view with the shadowy hulk of the wingless fuselage in the background. What a remarkable feeling! That image is forever burned in my memory.

"Even better yet was when we drove up to the aircraft and got out to find that most everyone was still alive."

Jerry Alsum remembered also, "When we got out of the snow cat to take that last reading, we heard screams coming up out of the dark forest below us! My heart jumped into my throat. All of the plane crashes we had been involved in, up to this one, ended up being fatal to all occupants. This was not expected. Major adrenaline rush!

"That's when we knew we had found the plane, but I couldn't see the plane or any people at that point. But we knew it was down below us somewhere. We then got back in the snow cat and headed down the embankment, no longer worried about how steep it was, and looked for a path to get us in the general direction from where we heard the screams.

"During this time, I got on the radio and called back to base camp that we had found the plane, and there were survivors. I told them we were closing in to investigate. As we proceeded down the hill, I remember telling Dave to go slow in case there was a body underneath the snow. We didn't want to crush it or push it out of the way.

"Dave drove very slowly, and as we turned the corner, our headlights came upon the side of the plane, and we could see people standing outside waving at us. It was blizzard conditions with snow blowing completely horizontal."

Don Niekerk recalled, "When we stopped to take another DF reading, we could tell we were getting close to the airplane, but we didn't know this would be our last stop. We had just stepped out into the dark, with the wind blowing snow past, when we heard people yelling at us. It's very hard to put into words what I was thinking and feeling when I heard passengers screaming, yelling, and crying in what seemed like the middle of nowhere.

"Seeing and hearing people standing by the airplane and then running to us in the middle of the night, in the freezing cold and snow, in the dark forest, is one memory that will stay with me forever.

"Jerry and Steve radioed the base camp that we had found the airplane and that we had many survivors."

Chapter 9

It had been several hours since the snow cat left the Grizzly Creek cabin, and the remaining search and rescue team could only wait to see what would happen next. They prepared themselves, and their gear, for whatever scenario might develop. The little cabin now had lights and heat and another page would be added to its long history on this frigid night.

Jim Alsum said, "We set up our base camp and waited to hear from the rescue team in the snow cat. Occasionally, Jerry would radio back and tell us they were reversing course because of the logging trails. We wandered in and out of the cabin, but Harry Blakeman pretty much stayed in his vehicle. Harry's vehicle was well equipped with radios and he focused on communication."

Harry positioned his vehicle as best he could and powered up the mobile communications platform. "I thought I could be of the most help by relaying critical radio communications back to Civil Air Patrol headquarters at Lowry Air Force Base in Denver and to State Patrol Communications Center in Hot Sulphur Springs and maintaining communications with the snow cat going out to search. Contact with the rescue team wasn't a problem even though they had only low power handheld radios with them. They were only a few miles away and higher up the mountain. We were all anxious to hear what kind of progress the team was making going up the road to Buffalo Pass, but I knew not to call them on the radio and interrupt whatever they were doing. The noise of the snow cat might make it impossible for them to hear me calling anyway.

"Occasionally, Jerry would call and give a report, but most of the time the news was that the direction finder was acting very oddly and inconsistently or that they had traveled down another road that dead ended and they were backtracking out. I had a briefcase full of maps—aviation charts, topographical maps, fishing, hunting, and backpacking maps, but none of them showed the logging roads the snow cat was encountering. It was difficult to tell where the snow cat team was located. I stayed in my vehicle almost the entire time with the engine running to power the radios and to keep the heater going. Only occasionally did I get out and walk around to keep my blood circulating and to clear snow away from the exhaust pipe.

"Communications with the State Patrol in Hot Sulphur Springs was marginal at times, but I always got through. The State Patrol Sargent who came to the base camp later was unable to reach the CSP communications center on his car radio and came to my vehicle and used my radio when he needed to reach his headquarters. High Frequency communications on the CAP channel with the Bergers and with Headquarters at Lowry was reliable but not perfect. I called the State Patrol and asked them to get a Jackson County snowplow to come and plow the last three miles of County Road Twenty-Four so that we could get ambulances in to the Guard Station if they were needed. That was shortly after we arrived and Flight 217 had not yet been located. Unlike the Wichita State University crash site, we did not have the advantage of a telephone. There wasn't a lot of information I could radio to the State Patrol Communications Center other than we were still searching and getting closer based on the increasing strength of the ELT signal.

"Eventually, Jerry reported that they had reached the top of the pass and were trying to get a good reading from the DF unit. We continued to wait, and suddenly we heard Jerry's voice on the radio..."

"We found the airplane and we have survivors! The baby is okay!"

Jim Alsum thought, *There's a baby on board? After a plane crash? In the cold and snow? Now what?* "We had never had a crash with survivors, much less this many. Now what? Thanks to Harry and communications, we soon had sheriff's officers, more rescue personnel, more snow cats, dozens of snowmobiles, and the press."

Harry continued, "The news that there were survivors definitely lifted everyone's spirit. Then I was busy having many conversations with the State Patrol requesting the additional resources we needed such as ambulances, snow cats, snowmobiles, medical personnel, medical supplies, rescue implements etc. As Civil Air

Patrol, we responded to missing aircraft incidents all across the state of Colorado, and it was impossible to keep a catalog of what resources were available in all areas. I didn't know exactly what kind of resources or in what numbers we would be able to get from Jackson, Grand, and Routt counties. Jackson was a small county, and I had worked with the sheriff of Grand County and knew their resources would have to come from the east side of the county. Routt County would have to send their help over Highway Forty and Rabbit Ears Pass, and even in normal winter storms with lower wind speeds, the snow would whip out of the meadows onto the highway severely reducing visibility and causing snowdrifts. All in all, it seemed like it would be quite a while before we got what we needed.

"Meanwhile, as a CAP Public Information Officer, I could provide information on Civil Air Patrol activities to the arriving news media and also relay information by radio to our CAP information center at Lowry Air Force Base. News media calls were coming in to that information center from all across the country. The county sheriff would provide information about the rescue activities taking place at the aircraft, but I had a 35 mm still camera and a 16 mm movie camera to document rescue activities at the Guard Station."

*****

Jerry Alsum described the crash site as they found it. "The plane was lying on its right side with major damage to the captain's side of the cockpit. The tail appeared to be intact, and other than the fact that the wings were missing, the fuselage was dent free with the left landing gear still in its original position. The captain's seat was empty and exposed to the outside and the windshield was missing. Snow was covering the remainder of the nose.

"We moved in another few yards and Dave stopped the snow cat. We all piled out and started talking to the people who were standing there crying and yelling and telling us how happy they were to see us. One lady was holding a baby. It then became a matter of assessing the scene to figure out where the victims were."

Don Niekerk said, "I went to the cockpit and found it full of snow and ice. Some of the passengers had dug the captain out and taken him to the baggage compartment due to his severe injuries. The copilot was still trapped in his seat. The passengers had found him completely buried in snow and ice and had only been able to dig him out down to his chest. The snow had packed around him so hard you couldn't remove it with just your bare hands."

Jerry said, "I talked to a young man who was a passenger—I later learned his name was Jon Pratt—and he said there were victims in the luggage compartment and also in the main cabin. He said they had dug the captain out of his seat and put him in the luggage compartment along with a couple of other guys and someone to look after them. He said they had emptied all the luggage and spread the clothes over everyone that was still in the main cabin to help keep them warm.

"Jon asked me if we had a hammer, or an axe, or some kind of tool that we could use to dig out snow and ice that trapped the copilot in his seat. I went to the cockpit and found Don talking to the copilot and trying to dig him out. Dave came up to help also. We moved some suitcases and clothes that Jon had covered him with, and I did a quick assessment. He told us his name was Gary Coleman, and he kept saying he was, 'So cold...so cold.'"

Don said, "We asked Dave if he had anything in the snow cat that we could use to chip the ice away, and he found a piece of steel rod and gave it to us. Jerry and I saw how very cold Gary was, and we needed to warm him up. We asked Dave if he had anything hot to drink in the snow cat, and he gave us his thermos of coffee. Gary was awake and talking to us the whole time. He had been trapped in the ice all night and we gave him the hot coffee and started digging.

"While we were working to get Gary out, the passengers in the main cabin could see and hear us. I remember looking back there, with the plane on its side, and seeing people on top of people. Some were still in their seats, but some of the seats had broken away from the floor. It was one big tangled mess of people and seats and everything else that had broken loose. If one person tried to move, another person would scream in pain.

"They had covered the holes in the cabin with luggage and clothes. One of the passengers had her wedding dress with her, and it was covering an opening to keep the snow and wind out. The passengers were begging us to get them out of the airplane, but we had to wait until we had more people and rescue gear. The base camp promised to send help as soon as they could.

"There was only room for one of us in the cockpit to dig Gary out, so Jerry went back to check on the captain and the other passengers in the luggage compartment."

Jerry said, "At that point, I handed my radio to Steve Poulson, and he took over all communications and did an outstanding job with that. Don continued working to free the copilot, and I went to retrieve my trauma kit. I brought it over near the fuselage so I could get first aid equipment out to start working on the passengers that remained in the plane. It was snowing so hard that when I opened up my kit, within like thirty seconds or so, it was covered with snow. I covered it with one of the blankets we had brought with us to keep it somewhat clear of snow while I rendered first aid to people.

"I started piling our equipment near the nose of the airplane to keep it organized and then proceeded back to the baggage compartment to assess the situation there. Once I opened up the door and shined my flashlight in, I noticed three or four guys sitting on the floor of the compartment with a man lying across their laps. He had a severely lacerated face, and they told me this was the pilot. I told them I would get back with them in a few minutes.

"I went back to check on Don who was still digging the copilot out and asked him to help me open the main passenger door. When we opened it and shined our flashlights in, we were met with passengers yelling at us to get them out of there. Everyone was lying on what used to be the right sidewall and windows of the cabin. They were shivering and looked tired and scared.

"The odor that we encountered was horrendous. The smell was a combination of urine, feces, blood, and snow all mixed together. It was a smell that stayed with me for many years and was easily triggered by any foul smelling object that I came upon after that time. We told them there was just the four of us, and we had nowhere to put them if we got them out. We were going to need a lot more people and a lot more equipment."

Dave Lindow described entering the passenger cabin. "The interior was pretty much destroyed with seats and people scattered everywhere. As I was searching through the cabin to see who I could help, I heard a voice that sounded familiar, but I couldn't quite find him as I didn't have a flashlight. From recognizing each other's voices, we realized who we each were and he kept saying, 'Get me out of here.' I finally found my friend, John Butts, under a pile of seats behind the cockpit and got the seats off of him. I didn't want to move him, but he assured me all parts were working and he was getting up whether I helped him or not. I helped him up and out, and luckily he only suffered a broken tailbone. I had no idea I would find a friend from Steamboat in the wreckage."

*****

Rod Hanna was the Director of Public Relations for the Steamboat Ski Resort. A former newspaper and freelance photographer, he had maintained a close working relationship with the wire services and Denver newspapers after his move to Steamboat in 1975. As such, he regularly submitted photographs from the Steamboat area for publication and was even provided with a picture transmitter from United Press International.

Rod remembers, "I got a call early that evening from Joe Marquette, the Denver photo chief for UPI."

Marquette said, "It looks like Rocky Mountain Airways has lost a plane up there somewhere. Can you cover for me until I can get up there?"

"Then I got a call from Gary Klein, the mountain manager for the Ski Resort, saying he had been asked to provide two of the ski area's snow cats to assist in the rescue. Klein was loading the snow cat on a flatbed truck and invited me to go along. Gathering my camera equipment and warm clothing, I joined him for the drive over Rabbit Ear's Pass to the now forming staging area for the rescue in the Coalmont area on the eastern side of Buffalo Pass."

*****

December the fourth, 1978 was a typical busy Monday at the Steamboat Ski Area. The slopes required constant maintenance in order to be well groomed and safe for the crowds of locals and tourist who patronized the area in winter. The corporation had invested in the special equipment needed for the daily task—including snow cats.

The expensive equipment also required constant maintenance to insure its reliability, and shop foreman, Bob Werner, was tasked with that responsibility.

Bob remembers that Monday evening and states, "After a busy day at work, I was at home when I saw the news report that Rocky was missing a plane. Early the next morning, the news remained the same, the airplane had not been located. When I arrived at work, Gary Kline, Slope Maintenance Supervisor, informed me that he and I were to take the two Ski Corp Tucker snow cats to Walden, and we would be instructed on the way where we should go to start the rescue.

"We loaded the snow cats on two flatbed trucks owned by Ed Andrews and Ben Kemmer. Rod Hanna, the resort's Director of Public Relations also went with us. The drive over Rabbit Ears Pass was like any other trip over the Pass in December—snow packed and icy. The North Park Road, Highway Fourteen, was black ice, and I was amazed how Ben and Ed kept the trucks on the road.

"We were informed that the search was being conducted from the Grizzly Creek Ranger Station, and we arrived there about sun up to find a busy but organized scene. Dave Lindow had already taken a rescue team up the mountain in his snow cat and found the crash site. We unloaded our two snow cats and prepared to head up to the Pass."

*****

Dan Alsum had been waiting at the base camp to hear from his older brother. "When Jerry radioed that they had found the plane and we had survivors, I asked him what he needed. He answered, 'Everything and everyone.' We had put the word out and more rescue personnel were soon arriving. We had requested more snow cats, and they were on the way. My dad assigned Rick Hopp and I to take our snowmobiles, along with the rescue sled and equipment, and try to make it up to the crash site to help Jerry. Dave Lindow's snow cat had left a trail of packed snow, and we hoped that if we stayed in his tracks, our snowmobiles could gain traction.

"We loaded casualty bags, shovels, blankets—whatever we could carry—to head up the trail to the scene. The snow was falling at an incredible rate, and it was still dark. The tracks that the lead snow cat had left were very confusing. We would come to a fork in their trail and would not be able to tell which direction they had taken. We would take a turn at a fork only to find that the trail led to the snow cat turning around or simply backing down the trail. Rick and I would have to get off our snowmobiles and sink to our waist in snow. The difficulty we had was that we had to turn the snowmobiles around along with the rescue sled. We would have to unhook the sled and then push each other out onto the packed trail. Other snowmobiles and snow cats would have the same problem deciding which fork in the trail to take."

*****

Steve Poulson was briefing everyone on the radio and communicating the urgency of what was needed at the crash site. Sonny Elgin and Jim Alsum had men and equipment gathering at Grizzly Station and were putting the new resources to good use. They informed Steve that the Ski Corp. snow cats were on their way up the mountain but were having a difficult time following the trail.

Jim Alsum was happy to dispatch the Ski Corp snow cats to the crash site. "We now had more snow cats and knew that we would soon have survivors arriving at the base camp. A gentleman, who I suspected was a news man, walked up carrying a large footlocker type box and said it was his first aid gear. I let him board a snow cat headed to the scene, and thank goodness I did. He recorded lots of pictures, video and stills, which were very good. He did not compromise the rescue and did amazing work recording the scene."

Jerry said, "Steve told us that the reinforcement snowmobiles and snow cats were having a difficult time locating us because we had backtracked so many times on our way up. We decided at that time that we should send our snow cat back down to the base camp with the walking wounded and the baby. We unloaded all our remaining equipment from Dave's snow cat and put it in the cache near the nose of the plane. This would give incoming snow cats a direct path to follow."

Dave Lindow added, "After a while, it became apparent that treating the most seriously injured would be easier if we had more room, so the walking wounded were helped out of the fuselage and the baggage compartment and were loaded into the cat along with the baby in someone's arms and I headed out." It was still dark but we made good time. On the way down, I found the Ski Corp snow cats waiting near the top of the east side road so they could follow my tracks to the crash site. The wind had completely drifted over my earlier tracks, and with the poor visibility, they decided to wait because they didn't want to get off course."

Don Niekerk said, "I remember watching the snow cat disappear into the dark, not knowing how long it would be before Dave or other rescue people would be coming back to help. After the snow cat left, Steve stayed on the radio and Jerry and I continued to check on the other passengers."

Jerry had similar concerns, "Don, Steve, and I were now alone on the mountain with no other help. When the sound of the snow cat faded down the hillside and it became quiet, I felt very alone and afraid we might not get off the mountain either, but then, I remembered that there was a lot of help down below, and we still had the radio to direct them to us.

"Don and I didn't try to do first aid on the remaining victims because of the weather conditions, and we didn't want to crawl into the plane and risk stepping on someone or cause them to have to move with broken bones. They were lying intertwined and on top of each other. When one person moved they all felt it. We did check to make sure no one was bleeding. We asked them what their injuries were, and to a person they could describe which limb was fractured or what other injuries they had.

"While we were talking to the passengers, we noticed one lady was not moving or saying anything. When I asked about her condition, they said she had passed away soon after the plane had crashed. She became our first and only fatality while we were on the scene.

"They kept asking where they were, and when we told them, they were mystified because they were convinced they were somewhere in the Denver area. When we told them that they were only about fifteen air miles from the Steamboat airport, they couldn't believe it because they had been flying for an hour, and the pilots had told them the flight to Denver would last about an hour."

© Photo by Rod Hanna

When the rescue teams arrived, they found the airplane lying on its right side and almost buried in the snow. The heavily damaged nose area and cockpit are to the left. The passenger entrance door and baggage compartment door is to the right with the transmission tower in the background. Both wings are broken off and covered in snow. The left main landing gear is intact and visible in the center of the photo. The initial rescue team found First Officer Gary Coleman still trapped in the cockpit by wreckage and impacted snow and ice. Using a length of scrap metal found in Dave Lindow's snow cat, they were able to dig him out and prepare him for transport. The rescue personnel at the rear of the airplane were working in waist deep snow.

© Photo by Rod Hanna

Passenger Luann Mercer was evacuated through the emergency window exit by Civil Air Patrol team member Jerry Alsum. Jerry is the gentleman on the left in the photo with Luann's right arm around his shoulder. Jerry and the rescue team carried Luann to the snow cat for transport to Grizzly Station where Dr. Larry Bookman had established a field hospital and triage center. Luann would be taken by ambulance to the hospital in Kremmling and eventually transferred to Swedish Medical Center in Denver. Her fiancé, Jeff, was being treated at St. Anthony in Denver and they would not see each other until Luann was released two weeks later. The amount of accumulated snow can be seen on the fuselage aft of the window exit. The rescue team in the background removed the critically injured passengers from the baggage compartment, including the captain, Scott Klopfenstein.

© Photo by Rod Hanna

This passenger is being transported in a down casualty bag and has been administered an IV. The IV fluids froze after a short time.

© *Photo by Rod Hanna*

Rescue workers preparing to evacuate injured survivors through the passenger entrance door. The evacuation began in the pre-dawn hours when Dave Lindow and the initial rescue team located the crash site. As seen in this photo, the rescue operation continued long after sunrise when additional snow cats arrived to continue the evacuation. The snowfall decreased as the morning progressed; however, the rescue workers were still hampered by waist deep snow around the wreckage. The crash site was located approximately thirteen miles from the Grizzly Creek Ranger Station where the Civil Air Patrol team had set up a base camp to conduct the rescue. Snow cat operators navigated the treacherous terrain in order to reach the scene and then transport the survivors to the triage area at the base camp.

© *Photo by Rod Hanna*

Once the initial rescue team found the airplane, many other volunteers arrived in snow cats and snowmobiles to assist with the rescue. The additional snow cats were able to follow the trail blazed by Dave Lindow's tracks until they neared the Pass where heavy snow and wind had covered them. Dave met them on his first trip down the mountain and directed them to the crash site. The deep snow made tough going for the snowmobiles unless they drove in the tracks made by the heavier equipment. In this photo, the fuselage is almost covered in snow, but the tail of the airplane can be seen to the left with the nose and cockpit area to the right. Fortunately, the airplane came to rest on its right side leaving the passenger entrance door and the baggage compartment door on top and available to be opened for evacuation.

© Photo by Rod Hanna

Rescue workers battled the weather conditions to evacuate passengers and move them to the snow cats seen in the background forward of the airplane. The powerlines can be seen above. Rod Hanna took this photo standing at the tail of the airplane looking forward. The vertical stabilizer is actually slanted to the right in the photo with the airplane lying on its right side. Rod was the Director of Public Relations for the Steamboat Ski Resort and arrived at the scene with the Ski Corp snow cats used in the rescue. His photos were picked up by the national wire services and transmitted to newspapers worldwide. The freezing temperatures actually helped control bleeding for the injured passengers, but it became an issue as they warmed up on the trip down the mountain. Each snow cat was assigned an EMT to treat those patients until reaching the field unit at Grizzly Station.

© Photo by Rod Hanna

Rescuers tried not to slip and fall in the snow while carrying a passenger to the snow cat. Most of the rescue personnel had been awake for over twenty-four hours and battled fatigue as well as the frigid temperature and deep snow. This photo was taken from forward of the aircraft looking aft. The open baggage compartment door can be seen at the top center with other rescue workers still taking passengers out and rendering medical treatment before preparing them for transport. After being placed in casualty bags for warmth and loaded on a stretcher, the passengers were carried around the tail of the airplane and then brought forward to the snow cat staging area. The task was not easy because the wings, engines, and other parts of the airplane had been covered by the heavy snowfall during the night and were now hidden from view.

© Photo by Rod Hanna

A passenger is being strapped to the back of an open snow cat for transport to Grizzly Guard Station. An EMT rode on the back to care for the patients during the long trip down the mountain. The Ski Corp snow cats were normally used to groom the ski slopes at the Steamboat Resort and only the forward cab was enclosed. When the resort learned of the crash, they did not hesitate to send the Ski Corp snow cats and their employees to aid the rescue effort. Bob Werner, Rod Hanna, Gary Kline, Ed Andrews, and Ben Kemmer transported the snow cats to the base camp at Grizzly and were all instrumental in saving lives.

Chapter 10

Dan Alsum and Rick Hopp found the crash scene in the dark. Dan said, "When we found the crash scene, the sun was just beginning to rise and the terrain was becoming brighter. I remember seeing the transmission tower and the airplane lying on its side. The first thing I did was find my brother, Jerry. We were glad to see each other. He asked me to check the baggage compartment. I proceeded to open the baggage door which was heavy because the plane was lying on its right side with the door facing up. People in the baggage compartment were looking up at me with an expression of distress. The smell was one that I can still remember today and have smelled many times again at other crash sites. I took one look and slowly closed the door to gather my thoughts.

"Don, Rick, and I were going through an EMT class with the emergency department at St. Anthony Hospital, we were probably eight weeks into the one-year program. In our short time in search and rescue, we had never had to deal with so many survivors of one airplane crash. I was overwhelmed."

Rescue personnel with far more EMT training and experience than Dan Alsum would probably have been easily overwhelmed also. The scene was isolated with some of the worst weather conditions possible and few resources available. The many victims had experienced severe life threatening injuries and had been suffering in horrible conditions for more than ten hours. Any experienced professional would require some time to process the overload of information and determine a course of action. However, experience was a scarce commodity on Buffalo Pass. Lives were saved by the heroic efforts of many people, but at dawn on December fifth, 1978, Jon Pratt was only twenty years old, Vern Bell was nineteen years old, and Dan Alsum had just graduated from high school a few months earlier. Rick Hopp was twenty and Jerry Alsum and Don Niekerk were just a little older at twenty-three. The passengers of Rocky Mountain Airways Flight 217 did not ask about their age or experience. They loved them all for their courage and determination.

Dan continued, "These people needed us and were in dire need of help. I opened the door back up and asked, 'How's it going?' I crawled inside and realized there was a pilot in there. *How did he get here?* I remember the passengers asking me, 'Where are we? Are we in Denver?'

"The pilot's injuries became our primary concern. All I could do was keep him stable and try to keep his airway open. The passengers in the compartment had done a good job of keeping him as comfortable and warm as they could."

*****

Don Niekerk said, "Just before sunrise, Rick Hopp and Dan Alsum drove up on their snowmobiles. It was so good to see them. After the snow cat left with Dave and his six passengers, I thought it would be many hours before other rescue people made it up to the plane. We were still working with Dave's steel rod to free the copilot. Jon Pratt and Vern Bell had worked so hard to dig the snow and ice away with their bare hands but had only got to his chest. The snow had packed in tight around him as it does in an avalanche.

"We had to use the steel rod like an ice pick around Gary's body and legs. I remember him telling us to be very careful where we went with that steel rod. He was so cold and we could not tell if he had internal injuries, but we kept him talking to keep him awake and alert as we chipped away the ice. Now that we had Dan and Rick to help, it went faster and we soon had him free. It took all four of us to get him out of the plane and into the warm casualty sleeping bag. He was beginning to warm up with the coffee and the sleeping bag, but we cautioned him to try hard to stay awake on the trip down the mountain. Soon after getting Gary out, snow cats full of rescue people began showing up."

Jerry added, "Once we got Gary out, we carefully placed him in a casualty bag, which is a down rescue type sleeping bag. The bag had a zipper that went from head to toe and could be opened from either end, allowing access to any part of the patient's body while they're in the bag. Gary was dressed in penny loafers and dress slacks. Once we placed him in the casualty bag, we continued to assess his condition, and he said he was so cold he couldn't feel his feet. We gave him more of Dave's hot coffee, and he said it made him feel somewhat better.

"Dawn was beginning so we could move around without flashlights. A little later, reinforcements began arriving, and then it was a parade of snow cats and snowmobiles with rescuers. At that point, I remember feeling relieved and because my adrenaline dropped, I began to feel rather weak myself. I sat down and just took a break.

"One of the teams that arrived was a group of EMTs with more equipment than we had. When they asked what the biggest medical need was, I pointed them to the pilot in the baggage compartment. They started IVs on him which I thought was odd knowing that it would probably freeze, which is what happened soon after they were started."

Dan was still doing what he could for the people in the baggage compartment when the reinforcements arrived. "Once the paramedics arrived, they also entered the compartment and we put the pilot on a backboard, stabilized him, and took him out. Once outside, I can remember holding a blanket over the paramedics to keep the falling snow off of them. We carefully packed the pilot into a casualty bag and carried him to one of the snow cats. We had to move the litter over the tail of the airplane in the deep snow. Going over the tail section was tricky because it was covered in snow and very slick. He was one of the first critical survivors to be transported. The task then became to assist in removing and packaging the remaining survivors. The whole time on the scene the snow was continuing to accumulate and cover our equipment. Keeping everything clean and organized was a daunting task in itself."

*****

When Dave Lindow descended the mountain with the six survivors and arrived back at the cabin, he found a much different scene than the one he had left. The small group of CAP folks had grown into a crowd of sheriff's deputies, medical personnel, more rescuers with snowmobiles, ambulances, and the press. They had been anxiously awaiting his arrival and rushed out to take custody of the surviving passengers. While they were being off loaded, he took the opportunity to stretch his legs and then prepared to go back up the mountain. After loading more rescue people and equipment, he pointed the snow cat back toward Buffalo Pass.

"We had only gone a short distance when the snow cat engine died and we came to an abrupt stop. We had plenty of fuel, and I knew it must be an ignition problem. After a few minutes of trouble shooting, I discovered a broken ignition coil wire. We were in a convenient spot to work on it, and I rounded up what I needed for the repair. We were soon on our way once again, but it occurred to me that if the engine had failed earlier, while we were climbing the mountain, we might not have found the airplane."

*****

Rod Hanna recalls his arrival at Grizzly Station. "It was some time before dawn when we reached the staging area and learned that Dave Lindow had found the wreckage right at the top of Buffalo Pass under the power lines. The authorities were holding the press, and anyone determined to be non-essential rescue personnel, at the staging area. After helping Klein unload the snow cat, I quietly settled in the passenger's seat with my cameras for the trip to the crash site. No way was I going to miss covering the actual rescue!

"Loaded in the open back of our snow cat were some dozen or so EMT's and medical staff needed at the crash site. We were still several hours away, navigating what is a winding road through the trees to the top of the pass which was now closed for the winter. By the time we reached the site, daylight was breaking and we could see the plane on its side.

"Getting out of the snow cat, as the EMTs with their medical supplies jumped off of the back, I noticed one guy who instead was carrying a movie camera. It was Tom Baer, who I knew to be the chief cameraman for Channel Nine in Denver. Tom had stashed his gear in a bag that looked the same as the EMTs were carrying and got on the back of the snow cat unnoticed. So Tom got exclusive movie footage of the rescue for his TV station, and I got exclusive still footage for the wire services and newspapers. Thus ingenuity carried the day, and we have a record of the rescue.

"Being experienced photo-journalists, we managed to stay out of the way of the rescue and each other. The scene looked chaotic with a number of snowmobiles and snow cats parked in the deep snow, but in reality, it was very organized as the medical pros went quietly about the business of extracting the passengers from the plane and providing needed emergency treatment, then loading them on the snow cats for the trip back to the staging area. This took a number of hours, and I later learned that a foot of snow fell during the rescue effort."

*****

Bob Werner described his role at Buffalo Pass. "At the time of our arrival at Grizzly Station, the scene seemed to be well organized by the Civil Air Patrol and the sheriff's deputies. We drove our snow cats off the trailers and then loaded men and equipment. The trip up the mountain was one of anticipation and fear of the unknown. I was anxious and on guard. I followed my boss, Gary Kline, as he followed Dave Lindow's tracks. The two Ski Corp. snow cats had open pickup type beds with room for one passenger in the cab with me. Dave Lindow's cat was completely enclosed. Rod Hanna rode in the snow cat with Gary Kline.

"When we reached the crash site, it was snowing and very cold, but the initial rescue team had the scene well organized, and everyone was doing their best to get the passengers as comfortable as possible and ready for the trip down the mountain. I backed my cat up to what was left of the front of the plane and EMT's loaded Captain Klopfenstein into the back on a litter covered with many layers of blankets. One of the EMT's rode on the back with him to provide what care he could during the transport.

"I got out of the cab to help and walked to the opening in the front of the plane where the cockpit used to be. I looked in on a scene of destruction. One passenger, an older gentleman, was still trapped in his seat on the right side of the plane against the forward bulkhead.

His feet were still entangled in the crumpled fuselage. By chance, I saw him a few days later being loaded on a Frontier flight in Hayden.

"I don't remember the name of the passenger in the front seat with me on the down-hill trip. I was so intent on getting the injured captain off the mountain and into an ambulance, I drove as fast as I could—being careful not to jolt my precious cargo. I got them down to Grizzly and we loaded Captain Klopfenstein into the first available ambulance which was driven by my friend, Walter Trout. I then headed back up the mountain to bring down more victims."

*****

Routt Memorial Hospital in Steamboat Springs was a relatively small facility; however, it could become quite busy during ski season, especially on the weekends. Doctor Larry Bookman normally worked at the level one trauma centers in Denver, but in the winter of 1978, he had also begun covering the emergency room in Steamboat on the weekends. He had been informed of the possible airplane crash on Monday evening, but no details were available. Routinely, he would have been back in Denver on Monday, but as fate would have it, he had stayed over an extra day in Steamboat.

Doctor Bookman recalls, "I received a call early on Tuesday morning and was informed that the airplane had been found, and there were possible survivors. I told the ambulance to pick me up, and we would go to the scene to see what we could do. Shortly after, I was informed there were several survivors and some were critical. We rounded up more EMTs and ambulances, and I sent one of them back to the hospital to pick up some advanced equipment that might be needed to stabilize patients.

"The weather was not good and we were probably in route for an hour and a half. We arrived at the small cabin at Grizzly Station after sunrise and prepared to triage and stabilize patients and then transport them. Conditions outside were not good, and I was amazed by the efforts of the rescue team.

"After examining each patient and stabilizing them for transport, the next decision was where to send them. I had not been practicing at Steamboat very long, but I knew what our facility could accommodate. I was less familiar with the resources at Kremmling, but the first survivors that came down the mountain were not critical, so we sent most of them to that hospital. I could only imagine the conditions at the crash site since some of the arriving patients were receiving IVs, and the bags had frozen. As more snow cats arrived and the injuries were more severe, I began sending patients to Steamboat where I knew we could handle internal injuries and fracture management. The most critical cases were transported to Denver General because I knew they could handle anything we sent their way, and they could do it immediately, including any surgery needed.

"At Steamboat we had one general surgeon, two orthopedic surgeons, and one nurse anesthetist. However, we only had one operating room, and I knew I had soon filled that capacity. We began sending more people to Kremmling. Once everyone had been transported, I hurried back to the hospital as soon as possible to further evaluate the injuries and initiate definitive treatment.

"Arriving back at Routt Memorial, I found the emergency room full and began to reassess the patients. Some were sent to surgery, some were admitted for further treatment, some were treated and then transported to Denver, and fortunately some were discharged.

"Looking back, it was a remarkable event with a way better than expected outcome, and I feel fortunate that I was a part of it and was able to help."

*****

Don Coleman and Ron Plunkett finally made it to Grizzly Ranger Station. Ron said, "Don and I arrived just before daylight. It wasn't long before we received word that one of the snow cats had heard the survivors and were proceeding to the site. Several snow cats came down before Gary was recovered, and Don and I got busy helping the EMTs with other passengers. I remember inserting IVs to help out because they were short-handed."

Don recalled the scene at Grizzly and said, "Right after we arrived at the trailhead, I got my tele skis on and took off up the road to the crash site. After a while, I heard a noise up on the hill. In the early light, I was getting an idea of what the area was like. I took off fast but slowed down after a period of time. I wasn't making much progress. It was too far to go, and I felt like I was on a treadmill—maybe going backwards. I never felt so helpless.

"It was so quiet, like it always is in the woods after a snowfall. The only sound was my heavy breathing. I can't remember what passed me first, a snow cat or a snowmobile, but they were headed downhill fast and obviously had a passenger onboard. I turned around and started to ski back. More vehicles passed me going downhill and then the first guys coming back after unloading. Now I was in the way and literally jumped off the road to avoid the traffic.

"Story of my life, trying to help, but… I realized help was here and I was actually smiling. An overwhelming army of angels had arrived. I needed to get my ass back down quick."

Ron said, "I was busy when Gary arrived—we overheard that they'd just brought down one of the pilots and hoped it was Gary. Don headed out to meet the snow cat. Ambulances were beginning to arrive, but only limited medical personnel were available. Gary was conscious but very groggy. Don stayed with him and kept him talking while I worked on seeing how we could get him staged for an ambulance."

Don said, "I helped get Gary into the cabin for triage and suddenly realized that one of the volunteers working with Gary was Paul Johnson, a friend of mine. Paul was a lead player in founding the Summit County Rescue Group.

"Seeing Paul was very strange. So many people at the scene in the dark early morning after such a horrible night. Then to see Paul next to me working on Gary. We looked at each other in disbelief. His jaw dropped when I told him the guy we were working over was my brother.

"I looked around to see who all these folks were. Where did they come from? Even Ron and I couldn't really process how we got there. The scene at the parking lot was surreal. Breath fog, blowing snow, snow plumes off the cat tracks rushing around, boots crackling in the frozen ground, barking commands mixed with calm caring questions. It seemed like time shifted to slow motion."

Ron remembered, "One of the EMTs I'd been working with joined me in getting Gary into an ambulance from Kremmling. It had an upper and a lower bunk.

"Don and I had down sleeping bags with us, and we got Gary moved to the ambulance and into one of the large down bags on the lower level with several bags over the top of him. Don took off his outer clothes, gave me the keys to drive his Land Cruiser, and crawled into the bag with Gary to warm him."

Don explained, "When I was talking to Gary in the ambulance, he was in and out of consciousness. I was a pain and kept him in more pain than he wanted to be so he wouldn't fall asleep. I kept asking him about the crash. He talked about the bright blue flash and seeing the clearing to the right. He described jamming the right rudder to steer to the clearing.

"In his delirium, lots of details were garbled or disconnected, but I kept him talking. The flash was very clear in his mind, and when I told him about the power line, he made the connection and looked a little relieved. It was too much to figure out on his own, but the cognitive engagement served to distract from the physical pain he had never experienced before.

"He asked me a lot about Scott. I told him he was in another ambulance, and I didn't know his condition.

"The whole thing was unbelievable. Going down in the power line was a big part of the miracle in my mind—the runway opening in the forest, the wing hitting the electrical lines, the big bright flash lighting up the clearing. The flash was more than a light bulb. It was long enough to light up the whole area. The wing must have rubbed the wire, or maybe the broken part bounced onto another wire that shorted. No one will ever know. The fact that the power outage helped triangulate their position was very interesting."

Gary had been buried in ice most of the night and his body temperature was very low. He shared the memory. "I only have a vague memory of being brought down to Grizzly Station. I remember the inside of the cabin and the pot-bellied stove and the blessed sensation of finally feeling a degree of warmth. I also recall the ambulance had bunks stacked in it like a military MASH unit, and I wondered where my brother, Don, came from and how he got there. I could hear the rattle of snow chains on the tires as Don talked to me to keep me awake."

After worrying all night, Don was happy to see his brother alive, but his joy was tempered by the fact that Gary was in critical condition and not out of danger. It was obvious that he was suffering from severe frostbite, among other things, and might lose a hand or foot or worse.

"It hurts to see one of your loved ones in pain—realizing that they might not survive. When we were growing up on the farm in Iowa, Gary was a concert clarinetist. He sat first chair with the Iowa State band for more than a year and then went to The University of Colorado on a music scholarship. Seeing his mangled hand when they pulled him out was so sad. The hand was almost translucent, as if I were looking at an X-ray, and I could see the broken bones. I knew he would never play his clarinet again—and he never has."

Gary would remain in the hospital at Kremmling for several days before being transferred by air ambulance to Denver. Gary's parents and Don would remain by his side.

Don remembered the transfer. "When the ambulance plane took off with Gary at Kremmling to fly him to Porter Hospital in Denver, I stood watching it disappear. There were so many questions still unanswered. When will they amputate his hand? How many toes will he lose? How many operations? Will he ever fly again? For that matter will I? Hell yes, we will!

"Mom and Dad were back at the hospital in Kremmling being briefed by the doctors. I needed to get back to Copper Mountain and go back to work. How was I going to explain all this?

"I never really talked much about the whole thing. Now I know why—it's not easy."

*****

After impatiently pacing around the cabin for hours, Jim Alsum became a very busy man.

"Snow cats were returning with injured, and the activity level increased—ambulances were coming and going. We used a four-wheel drive ambulance to shuttle patients from base camp out to the highway where they were then transferred to two-wheel drive ambulances. Medical teams set up a miniature emergency room in the base cabin where patients were taken after being off-loaded from the snow cats. They were evaluated by an MD and nurses, stabilized and then loaded into the ambulance. It was crowded, hot, and hectic.

"I stayed outside and directed patient movements. Many people pitched in to get the job done, and teamwork was everywhere. One elderly patient came down wearing a stocking hat that had some blood on it. It was serving as a dressing for his head wound, and he refused to remove it for any reason."

*****

Jerry Alsum continued his work at the crash site and recalls, "A group of snowmobilers arrived, and when I asked what medical training they had, they said, 'Very little.' They became the Quartermasters and patient movers. We then assisted the arriving rescuers with loading victims onto snow cats and packaging them for the ride down to the base camp. The cache of equipment near the nose of the plane became the loading dock area where patients and snow cats came together. Passengers were carried out of the plane, over the wing, around the nose, placed onto stretchers or stokes liters, covered with blankets, and then either placed into the snow cat or strapped to the back with rope. An EMT rode on the back to assure the patients' safety.

"We received a radio call from base camp asking us to do more bleeding control. We thought that was odd because they were not bleeding when we packaged them for transport. We decided it was too cold for them to bleed at the scene, but it could become a problem as they warmed up in the snow cat. Carrying victims from the aircraft door to the snow cats became hazardous due to the broken wing lying beneath the snow just forward of the door. Many rescuers slipped and fell on the wing. Walking around the scene became very tiresome because of the deep snow. I remember looking at some of the rescuers who were wearing snowmobile helmets, and they had snow building up on their helmets because it was coming down so hard."

Don Niekerk remarked, "I remember seeing the passengers side by side on the snow, all wrapped in blankets or in sleeping bags, waiting their turn for a ride to the base camp. I also remember going over to check up on each of them. I explained that we were just waiting for the snow cats to come back so we could transport them. Most of the patients rode on the outside of the snow cat, or strapped to a backboard hanging out the back, for the long ride to base camp. We could only get one or two passengers on the Ski Corp snow cats and an EMT to ride with them. Dave Lindow had the only enclosed cat that normally seated six."

Dan Alsum remembers wrapping up at the crash scene and said, "With the great work of the many different groups and individuals, the crash site became an organized loading zone of snow cats transporting the walking wounded and littered survivors to the base camp. Eventually, all the survivors were evacuated and all that was left was to transport the one fatality. She was transported on the sled that I pulled behind my snowmobile. Rick and I were saddened as we drove our snowmobiles carefully and respectfully. By the time we left the crash scene, the trail that we had struggled to come up looked like a well-packed ski slope."

Rick Hopp felt the fatigue once the task was done. "I'll never forget walking around that mess in waist deep snow trying to help everyone. I'll always remember taking turns chipping the ice off from around Gary Coleman to get him free of the cockpit. It was a truly life changing experience and one that forever embedded the value of life. Not only for those of us at the crash site but also for all the many who helped."

Jim Alsum concluded, "My son and Rick Hopp arrived last pulling the snow boat with the deceased lady. The base camp became very quiet and solemn. Once all passengers were transported, we broke camp and headed home. We arrived exhausted after thirty-three hours without sleep. I later discovered that my brother-in-law was at the Steamboat airport and scheduled to be on this flight but cancelled two-hours prior because of a change in his work requirement."

Sonny Elgin was similarly exhausted, "Once the aircraft was located, law enforcement had assumed incident command, and my job as mission coordinator was pretty much done. I waited for the survivors and the deceased to be brought down to the campground and transferred to other vehicles for transport to local medical facilities. I assisted where I could. I later helped the ground teams pack up their equipment and then headed for home. I arrived about seven p.m., almost twenty-four hours after the mission began. We were happy that the day ended with twenty-one lives saved and yet so sad there was a fatality."

Harry Blakeman remembers completing his duties, "As daylight came and the day progressed, the news media started arriving. As far as I knew, they had no way to get to the crash site from the Guard Station. I should have known better as I had been a very resourceful journalist myself. Once I rode into a search area with some CAP searchers who offered me a ride. Another time, I rode on a fire engine for several miles to get to a U.S. Army helicopter crash. There were other times when I was similarly resourceful.

"When all the survivors, the one deceased lady, and all the rescuers were off the Pass, I saw Tom Baer among the rescuers. I asked him where he had been and he said up at the crash site. I was astounded as I never knew he was up there. Tom and I had worked together at Channel Nine News in Denver from 1971 to about 1975. While I still did freelance work at Channel Nine, I hadn't seen Tom for several years since he was working out of Steamboat Springs. Tom asked if I would take his film back to Denver to be processed at the station. I also didn't know that Rod Hanna had gone up to the site on the other Ski Corp snow cat to take still photos.

"Rescue activities are ninety-nine percent somber, but occasionally there is a lighter moment. I recall a young, short female photojournalist from KMGH who approached me. I had talked to her previously at other news events while I was working as a journalist. This young lady must have grown up in a city. She asked if I could tell her where the bathroom was. I pointed to a cluster of trees behind the guard station and told her she could choose any one of the trees. The snow between us and the trees was three to four feet deep and there may have been a drift or two even deeper.

"The drive back to Denver was long and slow. I was exhausted even though I had not been to the site working on patients and wading through deep snow. Usually when we returned from an incident after working for twenty-four hours, we travelled in a convoy and talked back and forth on the radio to help keep everyone awake and alert. This time I was driving back by myself with no one to talk to, so frequent stops to get out and walk around were necessary. I couldn't stop for a nap as I was taking the news film back to Denver. At least the snow had stopped and the wind had died down and it was a much different drive than the night before."

Harrison Jones

*****

When all was said and done, Sgt. Jack Donner found himself guarding a quiet and empty scene. He had been on duty over twenty-four hours and was hungry, but someone had to secure the scene until the federal investigators arrived to take charge. It was unlikely anyone would be crazy enough to go up the mountain and disturb the crash scene, so he had retrieved his Highway Patrol cruiser after the road was plowed, and he waited to be relieved so he could go home. It was approaching noon, and the sun was peeking out between the clouds, but it did not make him less sleepy. Just another day in the career of a first responder.

Chapter 11

Don Coleman and Ron Plunkett left the base camp to accompany Gary to the hospital. Ron described the experience and explained, "Don stayed with Gary in the sleeping bag during the ambulance drive to Kremmling. I tried to keep up in Don's Land Cruiser, but it was really icy, and the Cruiser wanted to do loops. I think it was about mid-day when we arrived at the Kremmling hospital, and they rushed Gary into a room. He seemed to be doing okay—joking with the nurses as they were putting cool washcloths on his extremities to warm him. They asked Don and me to step out of the room, and we waited in the hall. A staff member brought us hot coffee, and even though neither of us drank coffee, we took it anyway to warm our hands. Eventually the doctor came out—he had a frown on his face and was shaking his head.

"Don and I thought everything was going well, but the doctor explained to us that even after several hours of time for Gary to warm, his blood temperature was still below eighty-six degrees, a temperature at which your blood becomes toxic. He informed us that he wasn't sure Gary would make it. Don called his parents and let them know that we had arrived with Gary in Kremmling, but he wasn't out of the woods yet. There had been some frostbite damage and more unknown injuries, and Gary was classified as critical."

Gary remembers very little about the trip to Kremmling or arriving at the hospital. "My first real awareness, after leaving the pot-bellied stove at the cabin, was lying on a gurney and covered by a sheet—completely covered by a sheet. I remember that I had been enjoying a conversation with my uncle, who had passed away many years before, and I had been playing with a favorite dog that had died when I was a young boy. For some reason, that did not seem unusual at all, and I was comfortable with it.

"Now my uncle and my favorite pet were gone, and I was covered on the gurney. I could hear two nurses talking and discussing the fact that it was a damn shame that someone so young had been lost. I didn't realize they were talking about me until one of them said, 'He was one of the pilots.' They were talking about the things they had tried to do to raise my body temperature, and they were not happy that I had died. I tried to sit up and said, 'When the Pharohs were dying, they would pile concubines around them to keep in their body heat. I think that would work with nurses!'

"One of them shrieked and went for the doctor."

*****

Bill Coleman was in limbo. "The calls from Mom and Dad continued till after midnight, still with little information to add. My brother Don and one of Gary's best friends, Ron Plunkett, had fled toward Steamboat where the CAP was headed. It was reported to be a wind chill of fifty below in the mountains, and each hour brought anxiety closer to dread. We had no idea what was unfolding on the mountain that night. We just knew it was bad.

"As I recall, it was about seven a.m. when dad called and said they had found the plane, and there were survivors. I will never know a greater surge of optimism. With the odds flipped to Gary's favor, there was new hope in spite of the image in my mind of what the nose of a crashed airplane usually looks like. The next agonizing hours were filled with reports being filed from various sources. Denver television and radio stations were reporting that they had found it and most had survived. It was declared to be one of the most incredible rescues ever by the Civil Air Patrol and the dozens of others who had volunteered to help.

"What was not clear was Gary's condition. We didn't know that he was found in a snow casket in the cockpit with his mangled left hand still on the throttles, trying not to crash the flying ice block that used to be his favorite plane on the planet. It must have been one horrendous storm of ice to bring Flight 217 down. When we got word that the rescuers had him, we didn't know that they couldn't find a heartbeat or that his body temperature was in the mid-eighties. We didn't know the fight my brother Don was in to bring Gary back to life. Not until he was admitted to the hospital did it become more clear the extent of those injuries, but hell, he was alive. Sure, his left hand was mangled, but his body temperature coming back up seemed to have left no damage. The dozens of other injuries paled compared to his hand, and I could only imagine my mother's pain seeing her former symphony clarinetist's hand in pieces.

"It was a few days before I got to Denver to see Gary, and I got what I expected. It was obvious that after seeing the flash of light out the starboard window when the wingtip hit the high voltage tower, and one hard turn to the right into a patch of tundra showing in the landing lights he had turned on, he doesn't remember much at all…a small but valuable gift. Gary healed up, but it has never left him. It stirs emotions when he thinks about Scott and Mrs. Hardin and all of the things that could have happened…and it isn't pleasant for him.

"I owe a great deal of gratitude to the amazing men who charged up the mountain that night and the caregivers afterward. I am proud of my brother, his skill, his judgement, and his tenacity for life."

*****

Rocky Mountain Airways Captain John Gottsleben was also flying that stormy Monday night. "Scott and I were good friends and lived in the same apartment complex. We both enjoyed skiing and would often take weekend trips to Steamboat along with our girlfriends. We had similar schedules that day, and so we rode to the airport together. Scott was flying the Steamboat route, and I was headed to Colorado Springs. We were due back at about the same time and planned to ride home together.

"Returning from Colorado Springs, I radioed dispatch, gave them our estimated ramp time, and asked what time 217 was due in. They told me to check with dispatch after landing, and I knew something was wrong. I stayed in dispatch, and we listened to the emergency frequency for anything we could learn which wasn't much other than the reports of aircraft picking up the ELT signal.

"When they brought Scotty to the hospital in Denver, I stayed with him and knew he was in bad shape. His parents flew in from Illinois, and I picked them up at the airport for the trip to the hospital.

It was so sad to watch them suffer along with Scotty. He never regained consciousness and passed away two days later. I accompanied Scotty's parents to his apartment and helped them pack his things. It was a gut wrenching experience, and they were just inconsolable. I felt so helpless. We lost a great guy and a great pilot."

*****

Maureen Redmond was happy to be rescued, "Dave Lindow, who was driving his snow cat, decided he should take anyone who was ambulatory down to the Grizzly Ranger Station which was on the Walden side of Buffalo Pass. I was bummed. I just wanted to go home to my bed.

"I think there were five or six of us including Matthew. One of them was the lady who had found Matthew in the back of the plane. She looked at me and said, 'That's my sweater you have on. Tell me where you live so I can come and get it later.' I could hardly believe it.

"Since I wasn't hurt, I just sat at the ranger cabin and waited for a ride to Steamboat Springs. There were so many rescuers around and not a lot for them to do, so I talked to a man who was a cross country skier who had come to see if he could help with the search. The search was now over, and it was just an evacuation. I remember telling him I hoped my parents didn't know about all this. I knew I was okay, but they would have been so worried.

"Meanwhile, my parents and my aunt and uncle, who lived near them, had a terrible night also. My younger sister had gotten off the school bus at the regular place, but my parents were snowed in and were not there to meet her. She walked two miles up the road to my parent's closest neighbor, and since she was underdressed and not prepared for the horrible weather, she was hypothermic. Fortunately, she had the sense to stop there and not continue on up the two miles to my parent's house. They put her in a hot tub and warmed her up and then called my aunt and uncle to come get her since my parent's unreliable phone line was down because of the storm. They settled her in for the night and went to bed.

"Back in Steamboat Springs, my two friends' husbands and my boyfriend had been notified that the plane was missing and were huddling, trying to decide what to do. At about three a.m., my boyfriend decided he should probably try to notify my parents. I think he was starting to believe this was not going to turn out so good and needed some support. Since the phone was down, my poor aunt and uncle got the call. My uncle had to get up and get dressed and shovel out of the driveway and try to drive up my parents' unplowed two-mile long driveway. He made it about a mile and a half and had to walk the rest of the way.

"So my dad answered the door at three a.m. to a frozen ice man who was crying his eyes out and saying, 'Maureen was flying to Denver, and the plane is missing.' Then, he had to help them decide what to wear, what to drive, and where to go because they were unable to think or move. My uncle loved me like one of his own children, so when I think of him during that ordeal, I cry. They got to Steamboat about nine a.m. and heard the radio station say the plane was found, and there were no fatalities, except they thought it said no survivors. They were so distraught, they had to stop in the middle of the street. They didn't know what to do but decided to go up to the hospital where they got the real story. They just decided to wait there until more news came in or I showed up.

"When the rescuers found me a place on an ambulance, they told me I was going to Kremmling. I threw a fit! I did not want to be on the opposite side of Rabbit Ears Pass from my bed. So I waited awhile longer and finally got taken to Routt Memorial in Steamboat Springs. I was a back seat driver the entire way. When you are lying down backward and can't see, it seems like you are going faster than you really are, so I kept telling the driver to slow down. I told him I did not want to wind up in the ditch after all this. I'm pretty sure he was happy to get to Steamboat and be rid of me.

"By then, I'd had it. I was hungry and tired and just wanted it all to be not true. My parents heard me before they took me out of the ambulance saying, 'Just leave me alone and let me walk!' They were happy at last to hear me complain.

"The hospital checked me in and X-Rayed my entire body and said I could go home. I was so scared that some part of me would break overnight that they let me stay until the next day. When I woke up the next morning, I could not even move my little finger. I was so stiff and sore, someone had to help me sit down, and lie down, and

131

stand up, and bend over. The high point was that lady coming over for her sweater…I still can't believe her!

"The airline offered me a settlement because I wasn't hurt and just lost my luggage. I actually found my empty suitcase on Buffalo Pass the next summer. I could not bring myself to fly for three years, and I still have to take Xanax when I do.

"When I look back on that night, I'm amazed at how matter of fact I was. I felt sure I would survive and was determined that would happen. I knew people were going to die, and I knew there were a lot of people badly hurt, but I could only think, *Wow, this is really bad!* I knew there was no way some of them could last very long out there, and I knew they didn't have the strength to walk out. I remember feeling irritated with the people who were crying and screaming thinking *Geez, you're just wasting your energy.* I wonder if I was in shock or if I'm just cold hearted.

"I'm not really sure what I said…if anything…to anyone, so I hope when other people tell their story, they don't say, 'There was this lady holding a baby who was so mean to me…telling me to shut up and stop crying.' I did confess to the Mercers that I was the one who used the wedding dress to keep the wind and snow out."

*****

Jon Pratt was more than happy to be rescued also, but he didn't feel that his responsibility ended with the arrival of the snow cat. "I got lost as a rescuer…when I watched the Channel Nine News the next day, I saw myself carrying a stack of blankets from the snow cat to put in the plane after all the rescuers got there. I stepped on the wing in the snow and fell on my butt and the blankets went flying everywhere. The news caption read, 'Tough going for the rescuers.'

"When everyone arrived, I got lost in the crowd, and everyone thought I was one of them. I was helping carry people out and doing whatever I was asked to do. Then, someone pointed at me and said, 'Ride out with the copilot and keep him awake. He has a bad concussion, and we don't want him to fall asleep.' So I jumped in the snow cat with Gary and tried to keep him awake. When we got to the cabin, there was a ton of people, and I got lost again as they all thought I was a rescuer.

"After standing around, they were loading an ambulance and it said Steamboat on it. I asked the driver if I could get a ride, and he agreed so I jumped in. On the way back to Steamboat, we were chatting and he looked over and said, 'Hey, what happened to your face?' I guess my swollen nose was beginning to show. I answered, 'Well, I hit the seat in front of me.' He asked, 'When?' I said, 'When we hit the ground.' He almost ran off the road and asked, 'You were on the plane?' He thought I was just another rescuer.

"It happened again at the hospital in Steamboat. He backed the ambulance in to the ER, and the two of us jump out of the front seat, opened the back doors, and unloaded two gurneys. There were over a hundred people there trying to see who the victims were. They followed the gurneys into the hospital, and I'm left standing there alone, not sure what to do. I decided to walk down to a friend's house to see if I could get a ride to the airport to get my car. As I'm walking away, the ambulance driver comes out with two nurses and a wheel chair running after me and telling me I have to get checked out in the ER. I did not sit in the wheel chair, but I walked back with them.

"The hospital was a mad house—I was the first person to show up who knew anything, and all these family members were just hammering me with questions. Patients were sent to three different hospitals, and no one had any names of anyone or which hospital he or she went to. The hospital staff was insistent I go to the ER to be checked out, but I said I would stay in the waiting room until everyone else was done. I remember sitting down at a table exhausted. It was about three p.m. and these people had been waiting all night and all day, and I was the first conscious person with any specific knowledge of what happened to the other passengers. I was surrounded by people asking if I saw their loved ones or even knew what hospital they were sent to. They would describe someone to me since I didn't know anyone's name, and apparently still in shock or from exhaustion, I would provide detailed descriptions of my fellow passenger's condition. This went on for a while and after one such insensitive graphic description of, 'Oh yeah, he had blood all over him and was screaming most of the night,' the family burst into tears and walked away inconsolable.

"A friend finally grabbed me and dragged me out of the waiting room after I had caused significantly more trauma than anything positive. She said, 'You need to come and talk to your mom, she's on the pay phone.' I can't recount exactly what I said to my mom other than I was okay. I do remember clearly the sound of relief in her voice.

"My folks and my girlfriend, Lois Grewe, had a rough night as well. The airline somehow figured out I was from nearby Estes Park, Colorado and started calling people with the last name Pratt out of the phone book at four a.m. After waking up another Pratt family and scaring them to death, they referred the caller to my parents who were then up the rest of the night not knowing what to do. My little sisters were still living at home and recount coming down stairs for school and seeing my dad sitting at the table with a glass of wine. A very unusual sight. My folks told them they were going to stay home today because of the snow, even though it wasn't a snow day. My loved ones, like so many others of passengers, received good news late that afternoon to their great relief."

*****

Bob Werner remained on scene until the rescue was complete and the Ski Corp snow cat was no longer needed. "Gary Kline and I arrived back at the ski area maintenance shop about eight p.m. that evening. Although Gary and I had not been up and awake as long as some of the other rescue personnel, the stress of the situation took its toll on both of us. We slept very well that night knowing we made a difference in the successful outcome of the rescue yet depressed that two fine young people were lost.

"A couple of days later, Gary Kline and I drove two Thiokol tracked snow cats back to the crash site to help recover the plane. I hooked a chain to the left main landing gear that was sticking out of the snow and pulled the fuselage out in the open away from the power lines. Then, a member of the recovery team cut the fuselage in half so a helicopter could lift it up and take it down to the Grizzly Creek Campground parking lot. Being a pilot myself, it hurt to see the craft cut in half. We moved the wings around as well, with the engines still attached, so the chopper could fly them out also. Any luggage left at the site, we hauled back to the ski slope maintenance shop. Some luggage was covered with snow and was not recovered until the next spring."

*****

Rod Hanna stayed at the crash site to photograph the entire rescue. "When it was finished, my ride with Kline was long gone with ferrying several passengers back to the staging area, so I hooked a ride with one of the last snow cats leaving the scene. Back at the staging area, I caught a ride on the back of a snowmobile out to the highway some eight miles away and then hitched a ride from there back to Steamboat. But I still had work to do. I met up with Joe Marquette of United Press International to develop the film, make prints, write captions, and start sending them out to the world. We worked out of a darkroom I maintained in our offices at the base of the ski area. So UPI had first choice of pictures. But as soon as the first picture went out, I received an angry call from the Associated Press photographer who was downtown working out of the Steamboat Pilot building demanding that I share the pictures. Wearing my PR Director hat, I agreed and shared a print that went over the AP wires and appeared in the Steamboat Pilot the next day.

"We finally finished about twenty-four hours after we first learned that the plane had gone down. Exhausted and running low on adrenaline but knowing we had been part of something extraordinary, the three of us gathered for a drink at the Robber's Roost, a bar in what is now the Sheraton Hotel at the base of the ski area."

Chapter 12

Airplane crashes in the United States are relatively rare considering the number of flights conducted daily. Accidents are even more rare when flights are conducted by the highly regulated airline industry. Federal Aviation Regulations cover every detail of an airline's operation and FAA (Federal Aviation Administration) oversight and inspection can be brutal to those not inclined to comply. When an accident does occur, the investigation is conducted by an independent agency, the National Transportation and Safety Board. The NTSB does not have regulatory or enforcement powers and can only determine a probable cause and recommend rule changes. It is then up to the FAA to legislate new rules and enforce them. NTSB investigations are detailed, comprehensive, and usually lengthy. Sometimes years pass before a probable cause is rendered.

In the case of Flight 217, the investigation lasted five months. Working groups were established for operations, air traffic control, weather, witnesses, human factors, structures, aircraft systems, power plants (engines), maintenance records, and avionics.

Participants in the investigation included representatives of the Federal Aviation Administration, Rocky Mountain Airways, Inc., DeHavilland Aircraft Corporation of Canada, Professional Air Traffic Controllers Organization, Air Line Pilots Association, and the Pratt and Whitney Group of United Technologies Corporation (manufacturer of the engines).

The wreckage was examined in great detail and all aircraft systems, including the engines and the ice protection system, were deemed airworthy and found to be working normally. Each instrument in the cockpit was tested and only the DME (distance measuring equipment) and one low frequency navigation instrument were found to be faulty. Those were known faults and previously noted in the aircraft logbook. The airplane was approved to fly with those maintenance carryovers, and neither directly contributed to the accident. The copilot's altimeter was destroyed. The captain's altimeter was in error but only because the ambient barometric pressure had changed since it was set at takeoff. The instrument was otherwise working normally.

The pilots were investigated and found to be current, qualified, and physically prepared with a legal rest period before their duty day.

The group of NTSB weather experts investigated the meteorological conditions at the time of the flight along with the weather reports and forecasts available to the crew. After five months of investigation, on May 3, 1979, a thirty-five-page report was issued by the NTSB. All factors involved in the flight were described in great detail and the following conclusion and probable cause was declared.

The National Transportation Safety Board determines that the probable cause of this accident was severe icing and strong downdrafts associated with a mountain wave which combined to exceed the aircraft's capability to maintain flight. Contributing to the accident was the captain's decision to fly into probable icing conditions that exceeded the conditions authorized by company directive.

It's interesting to note that the captain was not cited for violating a Federal Aviation Regulation—only a company policy. It's also noteworthy that the investigators did not have the benefit of interviewing Captain Klopfenstein with an opportunity for him to defend his decisions. First Officer Coleman, however, was interviewed extensively and was able to provide details of the flight.

The NTSB made two recommendations to the FAA following the investigation.

1- **Survival training for crewmembers flying commuter airlines in mountainous terrain.**

2- **Mandatory installation of shoulder harnesses, without exception, by June 1, 1979, on flight crew seats used in Part 135 operations.**

It is noteworthy that both Scott and Gary were well versed in survival techniques, but unfortunately, neither were able to use their knowledge nor experience after the crash at Buffalo Pass.

The second NTSB recommendation might have had a major impact. Had a shoulder harness been worn by the pilots, they may not have suffered incapacitating injuries and would have at least been available to help their passengers. One can only speculate as the NTSB did in recommending the legislation.

The FAA did make the new rule, and shoulder harnesses are now required on all flight crew seats. If you fly on a major airline, you will notice the flight attendants also use the required shoulder harness.

The detailed narrative of the report explains that the mountain wave and downdrafts were not forecast, and although the possibility of icing was forecast, the captain had just flown through that area with no problem. In addition to official weather reports and forecasts, PIREPS (pilot reports of actual conditions) are valuable pieces of information in a captain's decision making process. Scott checked for pilot reports before departing Steamboat and found the only one available was the one Gary made on the inbound flight. To Scott's credit, after encountering the ice and downdrafts on the outbound flight, he transmitted a pilot report to benefit other pilots and recommended no other flights should be made to Steamboat.

Decision making is by far the most difficult and important thing a captain must do. Those decisions are seldom made without considering all available resources, and they are not always made alone.

All airlines are required to have qualified dispatchers for flight planning purposes. Dispatchers are licensed and regulated by the FAA the same as pilots. The Federal Aviation Regulations state that the dispatcher and the pilot in command must both agree that a flight can be conducted legally and safely before it can be dispatched. Either can cancel the flight. In this case the dispatcher made his decision based on the same weather reports available to Scott. In fact, he made those reports available to the captain. The two men consulted by telephone and agreed the flight was safe to conduct. Neither knew about the mountain wave and downdrafts.

The NTSB agreed that the icing alone did not cause the accident, but the addition of the downdrafts combined to exceed the aircraft's performance capability. In fact, the accident report cited the aircraft manufacturer's certification data as indicating the following statement. "…under the icing conditions alone N25RM (Flight 217) should have been able to maintain about 19,500 feet at maximum climb power."

The report goes on to say, "…The captain had considerable experience in mountain flying and considerable experience in the DHC-6. Consequently, he was probably well aware of the aircraft's performance capabilities and its capabilities in at least moderate icing conditions. Additionally, he had successfully completed a flight through severe icing conditions. Therefore, he was probably not overly concerned about the icing conditions he might encounter with Flight 217 over the same route."

Later in the report, "…The captain was probably correct about the icing conditions because the ice accumulated during Flight 217's flight was not sufficient alone to have degraded aircraft performance to the extent that the aircraft was unable to maintain flight."

Once a flight departs, the captain is the sole authority for decisions concerning the operation, and the dispatcher becomes only a valuable resource. Every captain knows that with authority, comes responsibility and accountability. The authority and responsibility are welcome burdens that have taken years to achieve. The accountability is what keeps you awake at night.

First Officer Gary Coleman was found by the NTSB to have conducted himself properly and discharged his duties well. There were no penalties imposed and no criticism offered. First officers do not enjoy the benefit of command or authority, but responsibility and accountability are personal traits inherent to all good pilots and a burden that cannot be shared.

Gary Coleman was no exception. "After the accident, nightmares were a regular occurrence, and I learned to live with them. It was usually the same dream—a tree appeared in the windshield of the cockpit and passed from right to left—and then the crash. I survived and Scotty didn't… I can't reconcile why."

Gary explained that he was visited by the dream on a nightly basis for almost a year. He only gained reprieve after visiting the crash site and confronting the nightmare. At the time, he was dating his future wife, Debi, and she accompanied him for support. Finally, after reliving the crash a thousand times and asking himself what more he could have done, the visit to the scene of the accident allowed him to find a measure of peace.

Ron Plunkett, Gary's friend, opined. "Gary was copilot on 217, but he's normally the planner, leader, organizer, developer…giver, not the one being rescued. He knows he did what he was supposed to do as copilot that day…he just can't reconcile Mother Nature's impact or the loss of two precious lives, no matter how long he prays on the matter."

Chapter 13

Jeff and Luann Mercer did not make it to Florida and neither did their luggage. When friends visited the crash site in later years, they reported to Jeff and Luann that their wedding invitations could still be found scattered across the mountain. Jeff suffered a severe concussion as well as major facial injuries and has no memory of the crash or immediate post-crash events. He was transported to St. Anthony Hospital in Denver where surgeons performed several procedures to repair bone damage in the facial area. A lengthy rehabilitation and recovery followed. He never regained the memory of the crash.

Luann suffered facial contusions but did not have a concussion. She remembers, "It was a long night, and I was in a great deal of pain due to my leg injuries. It was such a relief when the rescue team arrived. The airplane was on its side, and I remember they had to lift me up to get me out. They put me on a snow cat and took me down to Grizzly Ranger Station."

The next day the front page of several newspapers featured a photo of Luann being carried through the snow by rescue workers. The photo was just one of the amazing shots produced by Rod Hanna.

Luann continued, "I was transported to the hospital in Kremmling for initial treatment and then moved by ambulance to Swedish Medical Center in Denver where I would be treated by orthopedic specialist. Jeff was at St. Anthony Hospital and we talked by telephone, but I think we were both still in shock and I didn't realize the extent of his injuries until I saw him when I was released two weeks after the crash.

"I had a compound fracture of the right leg, and my left leg was cut to the bone. It took approximately thirteen months for my right leg to heal. The doctor had to re-break it in order for it to mend properly."

On May 16, 1979, a young couple drove up to the front of the courthouse in Denver. The young man got out and fed coins into the parking meter, and then, he opened the passenger door and helped the young lady out of the car. He retrieved a pair of crutches for her use as she was hindered by a full leg cast. They carefully made their way inside, protecting the injured leg, and arrived at the appointed time to face the judge. They presented the requisite paperwork and legal forms, and when the judge found it to be in order, he said, "Repeat after me."

Luann said, "Unfortunately, I didn't get to wear the wedding dress due to the cast; however, the rescue people did bring the dress down to Grizzly with the passengers, and it was cleaned and repaired and as good as new."

Jeff added, "Directly after the judge married us, I busted out of his chambers running down to the expired parking meter where we were parked. The judge's secretary saw me running out and asked Luann if she was all right. She thought I was a runaway husband and deserting my bride."

When the *Wings Over the Rockies Air and Space* museum, located at the former Lowry AFB in Denver, opened a Flight 217 display of artifacts and memorabilia, Jeff and Luann loaned the wedding dress to be displayed.

Luann explained, "My father, Raymond Stubert, worked in the dry cleaning business, and he actually cleaned and repaired the dress. His name can still be seen on the repair tag attached to the dress in the museum exhibit."

*****

Margie Kotts Roosli had a similar experience to that of Jeff Mercer. Due to concussion, she has no memory of the accident. When a concussion occurs, any thoughts that have not been processed into long term memory are wiped out and can't be recovered. Thus, Margie and Jeff do not remember.

However, Margie does remember the events preceding the accident. "I was taking Matt to Denver to visit my sister. She had started a new business and was importing lambskins from New Zealand for babies to sleep on. She had decided to put a brochure together for the business and wanted to take photos of Matt on a lambskin. We ended up doing that at a later date.

"I don't remember anything about the accident, but I have heard bits and pieces about that night. Since I *wasn't there,* it was like hearing about a horrible thing that happened to someone else. I feel guilty about being conveniently knocked unconscious so that I did not have to experience that long night. I feel like I didn't do my part to help others, especially Maureen who had taken care of Matt all night. There are so many people who needed to be thanked for saving our lives!"

At eight months of age in 1978, Matt Kotts obviously has no recollection of his night at Buffalo Pass. However, it is a part of the family legacy and hopefully this publication will preserve the history. Ironically, as Matt grew up, he developed an interest in airplanes and aviation and is now a Certified Flight Instructor and flies professionally for a regional airline.

Matt describes the experience. "The crash was always a talking point growing up, and I was known as the baby in the crash. It was also a big thing for the news media—my grandmother, living in Switzerland, found out about the crash watching the news. I am the first pilot in the family and have always liked airplanes. I'm not sure if that's a byproduct of the events or not. When I started flying, my parents never tried to persuade me to do otherwise, and my mom even flew with me after I got my private pilot certificate. She has always been apprehensive about flying since the crash, and for some reason, flying with me helped her get over that.

"As I was building my flying hours and gaining experience, one of my jobs had me flying around the villages in Alaska where I experienced all kinds of weather, icing, low visibility, and a bunch of other situations that made it the most challenging flying I have ever done. There was more than one time when I found myself wondering if Scott was sitting there on my shoulder making sure I wouldn't do anything silly to prevent me from making it safely through the flight. It might just be a way of dealing with the concern, or I guess a certain healthy level of fear, but it was always comforting thinking of him being there sort of watching over me.

"I was sitting in ground school up in Alaska when the instructor analyzed a crash—Flight 217. He explained that the crash was the one that made shoulder harnesses mandatory. I told him that it sounded oddly familiar. He then told me that he was working for Rocky Mountain Airways at the time of the accident. We realized another example of how small the aviation world really is.

"I am also an electrician, and that was my vocation while I was learning to fly. Another ironic twist to the story is that my dad was a lineman with the power company and was involved in the construction of the power lines that we hit on Buffalo Pass."

In 2008, Ed O'Brien, a noted Civil Air Patrol member and historian, researched the CAP response to the crash of Flight 217. His research included an expedition to the crash site where he and members of the original rescue team were able to recover several significant artifacts and pieces of the airplane thirty years after the event. Ed was instrumental in the development of the *Wings Over the Rockies Air and Space Museum* display and donated the artifacts he had recovered. When the display was to be unveiled in 2008, Ed organized a thirty-year reunion for the survivors and the rescue personnel of Flight 217. Many of the passengers and rescue members had not met since the crash. Matt Kotts met Maureen Redmond for the second time in his life. He does not remember their first encounter, but it is a very vivid memory for Maureen.

Photo Courtesy of Don Niekerk

Maureen Redmond Smith and Matt Kotts at the thirty-year reunion in 2008.

Matt loaned his baby stroller, which he had recovered from the crash site years before, to the museum for display. It was also at this event when Luann Mercer loaned her wedding dress to be displayed. Maureen described how she had used the dress to protect Matt's mom, Margie, from the wind and snow on Buffalo Pass.

Matt was happy to attend the reunion. "I was able to meet Gary Coleman and a bunch of the survivors and rescuers and thank them all, especially Maureen Smith."

Maureen added, "I met Matthew and his mom at the ceremony for the CAP that was held at the museum in 2008. A few months later, Margie contacted me, and we met in Steamboat Springs for dinner. She had always been curious about what happened with Matthew that night. She is such a lovely person, and it was a very enjoyable evening. I am so happy for Matthew and his flying career."

*****

Don Niekerk and Jerry Alsum also loaned items to the museum for display. The Civil Air Patrol recognized Don and Jerry for their effort in the rescue by awarding each of them the organization's *Silver Medal of Valor*. The medal is the highest decoration awarded by CAP. The citation reads, "For distinguished and conspicuous heroic action at the risk of life above and beyond the call of normal duty."

The two were happy to loan their medals for display with the Flight 217 exhibit. Jerry related, "Don and I didn't feel that we should be singled out for recognition. We were a team, and the guys who were not on the first snow cat were just as qualified and just as important to the rescue as we were. The snow cat just couldn't hold all of us. We still don't see ourselves as heroes. We were trained to do what we did and voluntarily went there. The real hero was Jon Pratt. He responded to a crisis and probably saved lives. He didn't choose to be there but did what was necessary."

Everyone did not agree with Jerry's and Don's humility and assessment of their actions. The American Red Cross awarded each of them the organization's "Certificate of Merit" signed by President Jimmy Carter. They were also nominated for the "Carnegie Award."

They met with the Lt. Governor of Colorado and the national leadership of Civil Air Patrol for personal recognition and congratulations.

Jerry shared later memories. "One of the Denver hospitals the victims were taken to was St. Anthony, and my wife, Janice, ended up taking care of one of them during her clinical rotations for her nurse's training. A week after the incident, Don Niekerk, Rick Hopp, my brother Dan, and I went up to the hospital where Gary Coleman was recovering to see how he was doing. While there, we told each other what we did that night and tried to help Gary understand what happened during the crash, namely how the airplane ended up on its right side but had most of the damage to the left cockpit area. This was the second of many *meetings* we had with Gary over the years."

Don Niekerk added, "When we found Gary's room, there was a 'No Visitors' sign on the door, so we went to the nurse's station and asked how he was doing. We explained that we were the rescue team who had found the airplane and that Gary had been trapped in impacted snow and ice until we dug him out and got him into a down casualty bag. The nurse said the no visitors sign was just to keep strangers and news media from disturbing him and she would check to see if we could visit.

"When we were invited in, we saw that Gary's father, Harvey, was with him and they both had a lot of questions for us. His dad seemed really happy that we took the time to visit and I think we helped him understand what happened during the crash. They both thanked us several times, but we were just glad to see Gary getting better."

Jerry continued, "A couple of years after the accident, we returned to the scene during the summer and found pieces of the plane still at the site. The majority of the wreckage had been air lifted out later that winter by the NTSB. While looking at a piece of wingtip, we noticed a blackened mark at the tip and upon closer inspection, we noticed small parallel scratch marks within that blackened area. We discovered that this was the wingtip that struck the power line cables. Due to the size of that wingtip, we were unable to take it with us at the time.

"In 2008, we returned to the scene and found that same piece. It was no longer blackened at the tip, but the scratch marks were still there and we had more help, so we packed it out with us. Matt Kotts accompanied us on that trip, and we showed him exactly where the plane ended up. While doing that, we found an eighteen-inch piece of steel rebar lying where the cockpit had been. This was the *pipe* that Dave Lindow had handed me that night to dig Gary out with. Sadly, while being carried out in a bucket by a CAP cadet, it fell out without his notice. It's still up there somewhere."

Jerry continued his work with the search and rescue team for many years, and with his experience as an EMT, he later became a fireman/paramedic in Aurora, Colorado. As a first responder, Jerry has distinguished himself many times.

Don Niekerk accompanied Jerry on the visit to Buffalo Pass and took his camera along. "In the summer of 2008, a few of us who were on the search for Rocky Mountain Airways Flight 217, and other members of the Civil Air Patrol, went back to the crash site. We were joined by the youngest person who was on the plane that night. It was so good to see Matt Kotts after thirty years and to talk about what we did that night. It was great to find out that Matt is now a pilot."

Photo Courtesy of Don Niekerk

In 2008, the Civil Air Patrol team revisited the remote crash site and discovered the steel bar used to extricate Gary Coleman from the impacted ice of the cockpit. It was lying where they dropped it beside the mangled cockpit thirty years before. The makeshift tool was subsequently lost during the hike back to civilization, but fortunately, Don Niekerk had snapped a photo of the steel bar where it was found.

Photo courtesy of Don Niekerk

The Wingtip of RMA Flight 217 photographed as it was found by Civil Air Patrol members on Buffalo Pass in 2008. They were able to pack the wingtip out of the remote area and contribute it to be displayed at the Wings Over the Rockies Air and Space Museum in Denver.

Photo courtesy of Dennis Heap

The Wings Over the Rockies Air and Space Museum exhibit features Luann Mercer's wedding dress.

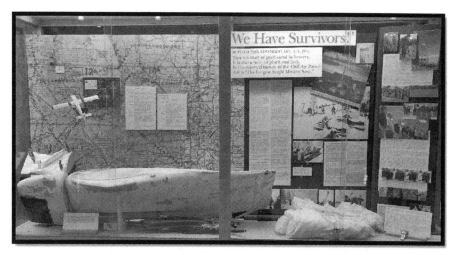

The Museum exhibit also displays aircraft wreckage recovered by the Civil Air Patrol rescue team as well as the metal frame of Matt Kotts' baby stroller.

*****

Dan Alsum reminisces about life after the rescue. "My part in this rescue was very small. Not only were there search and rescue teams but also the U.S. Air Force, Air Traffic Control, Sheriff's Departments, State Patrol, Steamboat Ski Patrol, and individuals who came together for a common purpose—to save lives.

"As I was growing up, my dad was a private pilot, and it sparked my fascination with airplanes and aviation. It became a driving force in my life. Today, as a professional pilot, I can look back at not only the Flight 217 experience but also many other searches and benefit from lessons learned. It seems that the aviation community is sometimes pretty small. In the summer of 2008, I had a corporate jet trip with a stop in Aspen, Colorado, and Don Niekerk was able to join me on the flight.

"While we were at the airport in Aspen, we ordered lunch at the Deli and gave my name for the order. When my name was called over the speakers to pick up the order, a gentleman came up to me and asked, 'What was your name?' I responded, 'Dan Alsum.' He stuck out his hand and introduced himself as Matt Kotts. Don had met Matt earlier on a Buffalo Pass reunion and recognized him. It took me a moment to realize who he was. I reached out to shake his hand and said, 'The last time I saw you, you were eight-months old.' Matt was now a flight instructor and was flying with a student to give him mountain flying instruction. Up to this point, we had never met. It's funny how this went full circle. I stayed in touch with Matt for a couple of years talking to him about flying and making it a career."

Don Niekerk was amused. He said, "It is a small world sometimes. It was funny seeing Dan's reaction to meeting Matt after thirty years. Matt and I had recently met, but Dan would never have recognized him."

Dan recalled another chance encounter. "Several summers after 1978, our team, which was now called Colorado Ground Search and Rescue Team, held our annual mountain climb. We were at the top of Longs Peak enjoying the view. We had our packs and Parkas with our CAP and CGSRT emblems on them. An individual came up to us and asked if we knew anything about the Rocky Mountain Airways crash. We said we did and asked why. He introduced himself as Gary Coleman, the copilot of Flight 217. What a small world."

*****

The CAP team members were not the only people recognized for their part in the rescue. Dave Lindow was recognized by the CAP for volunteering himself and the snow cat for the hazardous duty performed that night. Dave and Steve Poulson were also recognized along with Jerry and Don by the governor of Colorado.

Vern Bell was commended for his selfless actions on Buffalo Pass, and when he returned to work, his employer expressed appreciation for Vern's courage and determination in the form of a very substantial cash bonus.

*****

Jon Pratt was also widely praised for his tireless effort on Buffalo Pass. Jon received the following commendations—all well deserved.

- o A personal letter from President Gerald Ford
- o A National Search and Rescue Award
- o An award from ALPA (Air Line Pilots Association)
- o Boy Scouts of America Honor Medal with Crossed Palms
- o Federal Aviation Administration Extraordinary Service Award
- o Exceptional Service Award by Estes Park Boy Scout Troop Eight

Jon said, "In the fall, I was invited to a big dinner in Estes Park. I remember driving back from college on a snowy day to attend. There were about a hundred people in attendance, and I was presented a letter from President Gerald Ford, an award from ALPA (air line pilots association), and the Boy Scout Honor Medal with Crossed Palms.

"There was one other award from the local Boy Scout Troop Eight. It was just a troop awards ceremony dinner, but Gary Coleman was there and presented the award. It was the first time I had seen Gary since the crash. It was just a local event, and at the time, it didn't seem terribly important, but over the years that has become a very special memory for me. I think it was just too recent for us to really talk about what happened."

Gary also remembers the event and recalls, "When I was invited to the Scout's blue and gold banquet to make the presentation to Jon, I said it would be an honor to do so. The award was a very nice plaque engraved by the town of Estes Park, and it was my opportunity to publicly express my gratitude to Jon on behalf of myself and others."

Jon continued, "Almost two years later, in April 1980, I was invited to a FAA luncheon in Denver. There were quite a few people present, all in suits, and I was presented the FAA Extraordinary Service Award. The luncheon was at a restaurant right next to the runway at Stapleton, and my parents and girlfriend were there for me. My girlfriend, Lois, is now my wife of thirty-six years.

"In April after the crash, I left my job in Steamboat and went to Alaska, to spend thirty-five days climbing one of the toughest routes (Cassin Ridge) on Denali peaking at 20,322 feet. In hindsight, I realize this must have been really tough on my parents, who just went through the uncertainty of the crash—then to have no word for thirty-five days while I was on a dangerous climb. We were a week late returning, and my dad was apoplectic according to my wife and mom.

"Then, some thirty years later, I went to Nepal on a trek and to do some climbing. We walked out on the tarmac in Kathmandu International Airport to board the plane to fly into what the History Channel rates as the most dangerous airport in the world. Tenzing-Hillary Airport in Lukla, Nepal sits at 9,334 feet, and the runway is tilted at a twelve-percent grade. To my surprise, there sits an old de Havilland Twin Otter on which we will be flying today. I was almost sick right there and actually had to sit down on the runway. It took all my might to board that same fateful plane into the high mountains of Nepal.

"The crash of Flight 217 was an event that changed many people's lives forever. We all have memories that have impacted us in different ways. For me, it has made me appreciate my life every single day just a little bit more. The death of Mary Kay Hardin and Scott Klopfenstein is what has remained in the forefront of my thoughts all these years. While I didn't know them, I think of them and their families often and what they have missed. I only wish there was more I could have done so that their families would have had a full life with their loved ones also."

*****

The Rocky Mountain Airways fleet included six DHC-6 Twin Otters, and in January of 1978, the airline was the first in the world to inaugurate service with the de Havilland Dash-7. The four-engine turbo prop featured a spacious pressurized cabin for fifty passengers and a flight attendant to provide cabin safety as well as beverage service. The Dash-7 had been in service for almost a year at the time of the Flight 217 accident.

Debi Link joined the airline earlier in 1978 as a flight attendant, and by the end of that year, the company had assigned her the additional responsibility of hiring and training new flight attendants. Debi remembers the Flight 217 crash. "At that time, I was teaching a new hire flight attendant class. I received a call from RMA that Monday night to tell me there had been an accident and class would be cancelled the next day. I asked which flight had gone down, and the comment was, 'The one from Steamboat to Denver.' The plane crash was very emotional for me in many ways, especially because I thought my brother was on the flight. He was the City Attorney for Steamboat Springs, and he had flown to Denver that Monday morning to do some legal research. I knew he planned to return to Steamboat later that day. I was relieved to learn that he was not on the flight, but it was still such a sad event."

By the fall of 1979, Gary had recovered from his injuries and returned to flying status as a copilot on the Dash-7 where he encountered the attractive Miss Link working as a flight attendant. They flew together as crewmembers occasionally and exchanged jokes and small talk as flight crews are prone to do.

Debi explained, "I had spent the previous summer taking ground school classes for private pilot training and had just passed the FAA written exam. I was walking around an airplane on the tarmac in Aspen one afternoon when Gary walked up and introduced himself as a flight instructor. I had no idea he gave flying lessons as well as flying for the airline.

"Shortly after that, I was working a morning Dash-7 schedule, and Gary was the copilot. The last flight of the day was a Denver—Colorado Springs round-trip. While on the quick turn-around in the *Springs,* Gary called from the cockpit on the airplane's interphone system and asked if I would like to go to the University of Colorado Boulder football game after work. I told him I had to paint a room that afternoon. He said, 'I'll help paint the room tomorrow, if you go to the game with me today.' That got my attention.

"The return flight to Denver was bumpy, and after the passengers had deplaned, I began making my way up the aisle checking each row for items the passengers might have forgotten. When Gary came out of the cockpit, I guess he thought I was picking up trash. He decided to help and met me half-way with a few items placed atop a newspaper. I took the newspaper in my arms and pulled it toward me. To my surprise, two barf bags exploded and covered my jacket with a drippy mess.

"To Gary's credit, he escorted me off the plane to the side of the terminal where he located a hose and hosed my jacket down with great care and efficiency. Then, we went to the football game. Then, he gave me flying lessons. Then, when I had sixty hours of flight time in my logbook, I successfully received my Private Pilot's License.

"In late October, 1979, Gary and I visited my brother in Steamboat Springs. We took our hiking and camping gear and drove as close as possible to the crash site on Buffalo Pass. We backpacked in a few miles and camped near the site. The next morning, we continued our hike to the scene of the crash and found remnants of the event—part of the right aileron, luggage, and a baby doll. Gary confided his experience with the nightmares, and I think the trip helped him deal with the reality."

Eventually, Gary elected to leave RMA for more profitable endeavors and joined the family business at his father's request. Debi said, "Gary and I left RMA at about the same time. It was time for me to do something different but still within the travel industry. I worked as a travel agent for several years in Boulder.

"Gary did help me paint the room after the CU Boulder football game, and we were married two years after we met. After thirty-five years of marriage, you wouldn't believe what's on his *Honey Do* list now."

Debi and Gary still reside in Colorado. They have two yellow labs and a daughter named Kelly.

*****

In July, 2017, more than thirty-eight years after the Rocky Mountain Airways accident, this author had the privilege of interviewing Captain Scott Klopfenstein's mother. At ninety years of age, Virginia Klopfenstein has wonderful memories of Scott as a youngster and later fulfilling his dream of becoming a pilot. The family still lives in Illinois where Scott grew up.

Captain Klopfenstein's mom and his sister Jane reminisced. "Scott always said he wanted to be a pilot. He made this announcement when he was just eight years old. When he was in third grade, he got a "D" in math and his father told him that he would never make it as a pilot if he was not good in school. He went to summer school that year and brought the grade up to an "A".

"When he was in high school, he got a job at Elgin Airport and worked as a line boy fueling airplanes. He spent most of his money on flying lessons and worked with three other young men that also wanted to fly. To this day, we are still friends with Jim, Don, and Carl, and they are like family to us. We really appreciated them so much for staying in touch with our family all these years.

"Scott also had many other friends who were experienced pilots and lived nearby in Sleepy Hollow, Illinois. He looked up to them for advice and encouragement. Later, Scott attended Embry Riddle Aeronautical Institute in Florida for his college degree, and got his first flying job with a freight company in Texas. He flew the mail after that and also had a couple of jobs working for private companies flying people to various places in the United States.

"Scott liked flying for Rocky Mountain Airways—he was an excellent pilot and loved his job. He was also president of the Rocky Mountain Pilots Association and enjoyed being involved. He was well liked by everyone and treated people equally.

"Scott loved life...we miss him every day! We know that we will see Scott again."

Chapter 14

When an aircraft accident occurs, a wonderful machine is damaged or sometimes destroyed. As sad as that may be, in and of itself, it only creates a financial burden and an operational problem for the owner or operator. That is of little concern compared to the human consequence for the passengers and crew—mental, emotional, and physical consequences. The crash of Rocky Mountain Airways Flight 217 certainly created all those life changing factors, and tragically, the two fatalities changed the lives of all who knew and loved them.

Humans can only exist in time and place. A snapshot only defines life by a moment in time and geography. Being in the right place at the right time can create the opportunity for great fortune and happiness. Conversely, being in the wrong place at the wrong time can be most unfortunate. Time and place can create opportunities for heroes, and the same circumstance can expose weakness in others. There were no character flaws exposed among those aboard Flight 217.

For whatever reasons, twenty-two souls gathered at Steamboat Springs and boarded the Twin Otter bound for Denver. Some had made that decision long before December 4, 1978. Others chose to be in that time and place just a few hours before flight time. Still others changed their plans and didn't board the flight, thus providing that seat for one of the twenty-two who did.

Some would call it fate. Some would say it was fortune or lack thereof. Others might choose to believe it was preordained by divine intervention. No matter the opinion, twenty-two humans chose a seat and occupied that time and place. Each of them planned to be there for a variety of reasons, and each of them expected to arrive safely in Denver to carry on their lives in a pre-planned and orderly manner.

It's the unexpected events in life that creates chaos, and those same events sometimes serve to expose the true character of an individual. Panic, confusion, and fear are normal reactions to such events, and some believe that fear of the unknown is the most intense apprehension that can be experienced. There is no rational explanation and no solution to the unknown.

Few people have ever found themselves in more unexpected or more dire circumstances than the passengers and crew of Flight 217.

The two pilots certainly did not expect to find themselves in an emergency situation, although they were trained to expect the unexpected and to have contingency plans to deal with any circumstance. They knew of the possible icing conditions and included that factor in their preflight planning. The airplane was equipped to fly in such conditions, and they properly executed the established procedures for that eventuality. In fact, the NTSB established that the aircraft should have not had a problem with the icing condition. The following excerpt from the official report explains:

Aircraft Performance

According to the manufacturer's published performance data, a DHC-6-300, at a gross weight of 11,500 pounds with both engines operating at maximum climb power, can maintain an altitude of 19,500 feet after 30 min of flight in clouds containing a cloud liquid water content of 0.8 gm/meter^3 at -10°C with all deicing and anti-icing equipment operating. According to FAA criteria, exposure to these conditions can result in severe icing.

This performance data was available and known to both pilots as well as the dispatcher, and they had no reason not to expect the aircraft to perform as such. The mountain wave condition was unknown and unexpected, and the combination of the downdrafts and icing exceeded the aircrafts ability to maintain altitude.

Once they found themselves in the unexpected emergency, the decision to return to Steamboat seemed rational and justified considering they were dealing with unknown performance factors, and they knew the weather conditions at Steamboat were favorable. Once again quoting from the NTSB accident report:

"The captain's decision to return to Steamboat Springs apparently was prompted by his aircraft's inability to climb above 13,000 feet before arrival at Kater Intersection. He could not have safely continued beyond Kater without assurance that the aircraft could reach 16,000 feet within a few miles east of Kater...

"He probably was not aware of downdraft activity because of the comparative smoothness of the flight and the problems with ice accretion. However, under the circumstances, his decision near Kater to return to Steamboat Springs was a reasonable decision because it appeared his aircraft could not climb to the MEA (minimum enroute altitude) of 16,000 feet, and there was no other alternative airport available with an approved instrument approach procedure."

The flight crew found themselves in a time and place that could not have been expected and yet reacted without panic or confusion. It should be noted that by all accounts, they used every precious second of time to coax all available performance from the machine. They did everything possible under the circumstances to save the airplane and came within a few seconds and 150 feet of doing just that.

The passengers experienced a much different situation. They had no warning and no expectation of an impending emergency situation. Anything other than panic, confusion, and chaos would have been incredibly unlikely. Yet, after a normal reaction to abject fear and confusion, strong personal character traits and an indomitable human spirit made it possible to cope and not only survive but also to help those who could not help themselves.

Of the twenty-two souls on board Flight 217, two eventually succumbed to their injuries. Fourteen of the remaining survivors experienced serious injuries including fractured spinal columns, concussions, broken arms and legs, fractured ribs, and severe facial or scalp lacerations. Several of the passengers had one or more of these serious injuries. Only the copilot suffered frostbite of the hands and feet due to being trapped in the snow and ice.

Miraculously, six passengers only suffered relatively minor injuries. All six were instrumental in saving the lives of the more critically injured. In fact, even some of the passengers with serious injuries did their best to help others.

The true character and integrity of an individual is sometimes only exposed in dire, life threatening situations. Some people live their entire life and never discover what they are truly capable of. That worthiness can only be exposed in the face of severe adversity. Only then, can the depth of the human spirit be tested and the will to survive be demonstrated.

The survivors of Flight 217 were certainly tested. Their situation could not have been more adverse. They were stranded with few resources and no reasonable expectation of rescue in the near future. It was impossible to walk more than a short distance in the waist deep snow and hope could only be found within themselves and each other. It would have been easy to become selfish and ignore the plight of others, but instead, they shared the available clothing and makeshift blankets. There was no survival of the fittest attitude but rather compassion for the helpless. It would have been easy to take the resources from those with less chance of survival, but that thought did not occur to anyone involved. In fact, the most seriously injured were given more resources with the hope it would enhance their ability to survive.

The survivors were of diverse background and experience, and their ages covered a wide range, but they were motivated by courage and determination and they combined their knowledge and experience for the common good. They would not give up—and they would not allow anyone else to give up. Their story should inspire others to know that adversity can be overcome and hope should never be lost— no matter the circumstance.

Some psychologists believe that being heroic is genetic. That is, some individuals possess a heroic gene and only require an opportunity to demonstrate heroic actions. Those same psychologists believe the heroic gene enables one to change his or her perspective from that of being a victim to that of being a hero. That change in perspective greatly enhances the ability to survive. The opportunity for heroic action was clear and present on Buffalo Pass, and there were individuals among the passengers, the crew, and the rescue teams who accepted the challenge and fulfilled that need.

Tragedies are sometimes followed by miracles. On a December night in 1978, twenty-two souls inhabited a tiny isolated area of Buffalo Pass, without choice, and under the most tragic of circumstances—probably the most people to gather there in a hundred years other than when the power line was constructed. The miracle resulted in twenty survivors. Fortified with resilience and determination, they were able to survive long enough to be rescued and evacuated from Buffalo Pass in the care of compassionate men who volunteered and dedicated their effort simply to help another human being—with no expectation of reward or recognition.

One narrow definition of a *Miracle* is, "A highly improbable or extraordinary event, development, or accomplishment that brings very welcome consequences."

Aviation history is sprinkled with such incidents. There was the miracle on the Hudson when Captain Chesly Sullenberger and crew landed a U S Airways Airbus in the Hudson River after both engines failed. Another example has been called the Gimli Glider. That incident occurred when Captain Bob Pearson and crew were forced to land their Air Canada Boeing 767 at an abandoned airstrip in Gimli, Manitoba with dual engine failure. Both incidents occurred in relatively good weather. The miracle on Buffalo Pass was no less of a challenge for Captain Scott Klopfenstein and First Officer Gary Coleman. They were forced to land the Rocky Mountain Airways Twin Otter in mountainous terrain with very limited visibility and blizzard conditions.

On rare occasions, an event occurs that is reported worldwide and resonates with everyone who hears or reads the details. The true story of the passengers, crew, and rescue personnel of Rocky Mountain Airways Flight 217 was such an event. The *Miracle on Buffalo Pass* serves to inspire and encourage others to realize that with courage, determination, and compassion adversity can be defeated.

The crash site on Buffalo Pass is isolated and primitive. It is surrounded by wilderness, although thousands of airline passengers fly overhead every day. To those high flying passengers, it's just another mountain, although a sharp pilot might occasionally click the PA switch to announce the significance of the Continental Divide.

Months, and maybe years, pass without the presence of a single human being at the crash site unless a power company employee inspects the transmission lines, and that is normally accomplished with aircraft or drones.

Summer days can be peaceful and tranquil on the Pass, but when winter arrives, storms rage and snow accumulates in copious volume. Mountain wave winds howl at hurricane force, and the ice laden power lines hum their eerie high voltage song—but no one hears.

Made in the USA
Columbia, SC
24 January 2018